Praise for *Reading for Our Lives*

"I have rarely had as visceral a reaction to a book as I had in reading Maya Smart's brilliant and life-changing *Reading for Our Lives*. Like her namesake Maya Angelou, who suffered childhood trauma and couldn't speak, only to become a world-class orator and writer, Maya Smart helps us to navigate the perilous but fulfilling route from birth to literacy in the first six years of life. This is a book that every parent must read to make sure their children reach their full potential as readers and citizens of our nation."

—**Michael Eric Dyson, coauthor of *Unequal: A Story of America***

"A *must-read* for any parent! This exceptional book walks you through not only the *why* of reading to your child but the *way*. The scientifically grounded, step-by-step insights outlined here can heighten both your and your child's joy at learning one of life's most important skills: reading."

—**Barbara Oakley, author of *A Mind for Numbers***

"I anticipate a revolution of reading readiness once parents get their hands on this book! Preparing children at home so that they are equipped for school is a gift any parent can easily give with Smart's book in hand. I'll be recommending *Reading for Our Lives* for years to come. It's the best book about learning to read I've ever read!"

—**Julie Bogart, creator and founder of Brave Writer, author of *The Brave Learner* and *Raising Critical Thinkers***

"An amazing book for perhaps the most important job parents have: getting our kids to love to read."

—**Ryan Holiday, #1 *New York Times* bestselling author of *The Daily Stoic*, *The Obstacle Is the Way*, and *Ego Is the Enemy***

"This book is a wonderful resource for families with young children as it recognizes them as the child's 'first teachers.' It weaves together an introduction to early literacy through the child's ages and stages with recommendations that support raising a reader!"

—**Ann McClain Terrell, early childhood education consultant and National Association for the Education of Young Children past president**

"*Reading for Our Lives* is the book to turn to when nurturing critical readers. Like reading, Smart's book is for our children's lives. Don't miss out, because our kids must not miss out on the life-giving power of reading."

—**Ibram X. Kendi, National Book Award–winning author of *Stamped from the Beginning* and *How to Be an Antiracist***

READING FOR OUR LIVES

A Literacy Action Plan from Birth to Six

Maya Payne Smart

AVERY

an imprint of Penguin Random House
New York

AVERY

an imprint of Penguin Random House LLC
penguinrandomhouse.com

Excerpt from poem "Book Power" by Gwendolyn Brooks on page 24 reprinted by
Consent of Brooks Permissions.

Most Avery books are available at special quantity discounts for bulk purchase for sales
promotions, premiums, fund-raising, and educational needs. Special books or book
excerpts also can be created to fit specific needs. For details, write
SpecialMarkets@penguinrandomhouse.com.

Library of Congress Cataloging-in-Publication Data

Names: Smart, Maya Payne, author.
Title: Reading for our lives: a literacy action plan from birth to six / Maya Payne Smart.
Description: New York: Avery, Penguin Random House LLC, 2022. | Includes index.
Identifiers: LCCN 2022010712 (print) | LCCN 2022010713 (ebook) |
ISBN 9780593332177 (hardcover) | ISBN 9780593332184 (epub)
Subjects: LCSH: Reading (Elementary). | Children—Books and reading. |
Readiness for school.
Classification: LCC LB1573.S67 2022 (print) | LCC LB1573 (ebook) |
DDC 372.4—dc23/eng/20220425
LC record available at https://lccn.loc.gov/2022010712
LC ebook record available at https://lccn.loc.gov/2022010713

Printed in the United States of America
1st Printing

Book design by Silverglass Studio

For Zora, my daughter and inspiration.
Without you, this book would surely not exist.

CONTENTS

We Should All Be Readers

The question is not whether we can afford to invest in every child; it is whether we can afford not to.

—Marian Wright Edelman

The Quiet Crisis

Heavy rain once filled our local water supply with so much silt and debris that treatment systems failed. For the next seven days, local authorities and media raised the alarm that residents should boil their water or risk illness. Restaurants shut down. Families bought bottled water by the shelf-full. Hospitals procured truckloads of certified water and switched operating rooms to alternative sterilization methods. Once the boil notice was lifted, we all flushed our pipes, dumped ice machines, and resumed life and work as usual.

The crisis was obvious and urgent. The response clear and immediate. The end apparent.

What's happening with our nation's pipeline to reading, if you can call it that, is just as urgent, yet hidden. There is no infrastructure in place to raise a nation of readers, let alone a coordinated response to breakdowns.

Judged by international standards, two disturbing findings characterize U.S. adult literacy in recent decades: basic skills are weak overall (despite relatively high levels of education) and unusually persistent across generations. About one in six U.S. adults has low literacy skills, compared to, for example, one in twenty in Japan. That's approximately 36 million U.S. adults (roughly equal to the combined populations of New York, Michigan, and Minnesota) who can't compare and contrast written information, make low-level inferences, or locate information within a multipart document. And, worse still, socially disadvantaged parents in the U.S., compared to those in other countries, are more likely to pass on weaker skills to their children.

Completing medical forms, reading prescription instructions, parsing a voting ballot, and grasping employment or housing contract details are all challenging, if not impossible, tasks for far too many. The huge disconnect between the reading skills many Americans have and those they *need* affects their health, wellness, employment, housing, and even likelihood of incarceration.

But here's the part that all parents must understand: this crisis brews early. Much of the tragedy of low adult literacy has its roots in infancy, when early experiences launch lifelong learning trajectories. During this time, more than a million new neural connections are formed per second, and future brain development rests on the soundness or fragility of those earliest links. In fact, evidence from anatomical, physiological, and gene-expression studies all suggest that basic brain architecture is in place by around 2 years old and later brain development is mostly about refining "the major circuits and networks that are already established." And, critically, it's caregivers' nurturing, supportive back-and-forth verbal engagement in a child's first years that literally stimulates brain function and shapes brain structure.

For too long, as a nation we've tested school-aged kids, reported the results, and acted like oversight is a reading achievement delivery system. But literacy doesn't flow from federal mandates through state assessments and district policy to classroom instruction and students' brains. Standardized assessments are valuable, but limited, *alert* systems. Mere indicators, they can sound when our educational system fails to meet certain expectations. But they don't illuminate the root causes of that failure or tell us what to do about them. Alarms ring; they don't teach. And often when an alarm rings for too long, we tune it out.

Today, alarms abound. In the U.S., 5-year-olds have "significantly lower" emergent literacy than kids in other countries that have comprehensive early-childhood education and national paid parental leave. In a 2019 reading assessment, only one-third of a nationally representative sample of U.S. fourth- and eighth-grade students scored at a proficient level. Reading scores of the lowest-performing 9- and 13-year-olds have dropped since 2012. And—most devastatingly—just 14 percent of U.S. 15-year-olds read well enough to comprehend lengthy texts, handle abstract or counterintuitive concepts, and evaluate content and information sources to separate fact from opinion.

And don't even get me started on the state of children's reading interest and enjoyment. National surveys reveal skyrocketing percentages of 13-year-olds who say they "never or hardly ever" read for fun—29 percent in 2020, compared with 8 percent in 1984.

The sad truth is this: for the past few decades, the majority of American kids have been shuffled from grade to grade without ever reading well enough. And we're not talking about children with profound learning or intellectual disabilities. These are capable students whose reading development is hobbled by a devastating mix of untapped opportunity at home and inadequate instruction in schools.

Incredibly, that's despite the fact that elementary schools devote more time to English, reading, and language arts than anything else—often more than 30 percent of instructional time. Teachers struggle to meet the diverse needs of learners who arrive in their classrooms with little knowledge of the alphabet, the sounds of English, and the relationships between letters and sounds. They have trouble instilling these basics, let alone expanding the oral-language development, vocabulary, and background knowledge that allows kids to decode and comprehend words in print.

We can't afford to continue pretending that a hodgepodge of reactivity and remediation can get millions of children reading well enough to flourish. We can't leave whole populations without the skills, knowledge, and community support that underpin full participation in society and expect things to turn out well for them or for us. We all suffer when we don't muster the collective will, skill, and integrity to ensure that every child learns to read.

To attain the consciousness, solidarity, and equity our society so desperately needs, we must be informed and deliberate in nourishing early literacy. So, too, if we are to engender the level of citizenship, critical thinking, and limitless potential that our children and society deserve. And because the odds of success are set before school begins, we've got to start at home.

Parents and early caregivers hold the key. Period. We will never see the promise of mass literacy fulfilled until parents—our children's first teachers—understand how reading skills develop and how to spur them along.

The Missing Manual

Parents know that our children need to be strong readers to navigate school—and life—and we want to help them thrive. We know that we have a role to play, whether it's reading aloud to our kids, teaching them the alphabet, or helping them sound out words. But we tend to be fuzzy on the specifics and aren't sure that we have the knowledge to impart the right skills, the right way, at the right time. We worry that what we're doing now might not adequately prepare our children for what they'll need later. We crave validation that we and they are on track.

Concerns like these are justified, especially given the heightened demands of today's global society and post-industrial economy. We've experienced for ourselves the crucible of continuous learning, training, and development to garner new skills and master new technology amid constant change and new complexities. Who knows what future skills our little ones will need?

Parents frequently tell me they feel stretched too thin by the growing and competing demands of work, education, and family. They struggle to consistently find the time or energy to help their children move toward reading and writing (or, later, reading and writing *better*). They say things like:

> "I feel consumed by the basics—working, feeding the family, managing the calendar, shuttling everyone here and there. Getting my daughter ready for kindergarten isn't making the list."
>
> "There's so much conflicting advice out there. I have no idea what's best. I constantly question myself, wondering, 'Am I doing this right?'"
>
> "My energy is all tapped out. I fall asleep trying to read bedtime stories every night and worry that I'm failing my son."
>
> "I'm in the house 24/7 with my kids, but the quality's not there. I know I can do better; I just need to know how."

"I try to talk to my baby all day and read to her every night, but I'm just not sure the effort makes a difference."

"I want to play with my kids, not lecture and teach all the time, but I feel pressure to plan lessons and make everything educational."

Do any of these statements sound familiar? If so, this book is for you. I wrote it for parents who know that reading skills matter and who want to play a thoughtful, active, and effective role in nurturing them in their kids. I'll show you what to do at home, as well as how to advocate for high-quality instruction when your child goes to school. With this book in hand, your raise-a-reader education has begun.

My Journey

On the night my dad died, I walked to his bedside to show him a black-and-white sonogram, glossy and blurred. It may have been the first time I ever approached him while he was lying down. In my memories, he was always up—reading the newspaper at the kitchen table, mowing the lawn or shoveling snow, laboring over files in his office, watching some dark TV drama. I remember the picture feeling light and flimsy in the enormity of the moment, a father on his deathbed hearing his only child tell of the life she carried.

He took in the sound waves rendered in print, smiled, and whispered, *I think it's a boy, but I hope it's a girl.* He got his wish, but I never got to ask him what he meant by it. He passed within hours of his quiet declaration and left me to puzzle over the spaces between a parent's dreams and a child's promise, between presence and absence, between birth and legacy.

When our baby girl was born months later, my husband and I named her after Zora Neale Hurston to foretell a wise, bold, and colorful life. Like my parents did when they named me after Maya Angelou, we set the intention of resilience, fortitude, and distinction upon her young shoulders. We vowed to help our Zora experience the fullness of her inheritance—to discover herself as powerful, unique, and inseparable from all the life that pulses everywhere. Or, as her namesake put it, to know that each of us is "the world and the heavens boiled down to a drop."

I made reading—the miracle of connecting with others across space and time—a pillar of my mothering. In our first days at home, the intimacy of sharing stories and books became a touchstone. I recited lines from Jabari Asim's *Girl of Mine* from dawn till dusk. *Giggly, wiggly precious pearl. I'm so glad that you're my girl.* That little board book held my dreams for my daughter, held my awe of her existence. Reading it over and over felt like love and life support for a sleep-deprived mom. Soon I'd memorized the text, turning the pages only for show as I kept on rocking, reading, feeding her.

As a new mom who'd just lost a parent, I was comforted by the story's easy rhythms and my own belief in the power of a parent's words in a child's ear. Knowing firsthand how words nourish, I wanted to feed her page upon page, give her tastes of poetry, let her sip prose. I felt the book's upbeat refrain bolster something precious and fragile in her—and in me. Reading to her was love, care, and a pathway to a family ethos that I treasured. Toni Morrison said, "We die. That may be the meaning of life. But we do language. That may be the measure of our lives."

Stories were our first, most cherished language. I threw myself into the quest to raise a reader with all the zeal of new motherhood and the passion of someone who has lived the written word's power to both uplift and inspire. Soon, though, I was ready to expand my repertoire of literacy-promoting activities. But what to add? The advice in the books on my shelf, and in the articles I consumed voraciously, seemed to start and stop with storytime.

I put Zora in a Montessori toddler program for some professional backup. There, she gained other valuable skills through baby-doll washing and moving pompoms from one dish to another with tongs. Her fine-motor skills, potty training, and home tidying abilities blossomed, but I remained unsure about her reading development. Were the verbal experiences, social interactions, and classroom read-alouds enough? Was I doing my part at home?

The knowledge that parents need about reading development and instruction is not easy to come by. The U.S. invests little in children in their first few years of life, when the brain is at its most flexible to build a foundation for learning, social engagement, and health. There's no mass early-literacy boot camp for parents, valuable research is locked behind paywalls and inaccessible to the public, and too few experts communicate their findings in clear, understandable, and practical terms. Most librarians and booksellers are pros at helping us locate what they've stocked, but less adept at explaining how to facilitate language and literacy learning at different ages and stages.

I remember wandering the aisles of bookstores selecting the "best," most beautiful picture books for my newborn. I knew she couldn't lift her head or even see well yet. But I didn't know that a photo of a human face or a bold pattern would catch her attention more than the lush illustrations of a Caldecott Medal winner. And while I knew to talk to my baby, I didn't get that it was a two-way street from day one, that her coos and babbles were as significant as the words I spoke.

In short, I made every mistake in the book—if there had been such a book. Oh, how I wished there were a book (maybe with a title like *What to Deliver after You've Delivered*), preferably with a job description, manual of procedures, and performance metrics. But like so much of parenting, no clear instructions came with the position.

So I went back to school myself, enrolling in a graduate course at the Curry School of Education at the University of Virginia to get the literacy lowdown. I learned that there was more—much more— that I could do to unlock long-term reading and educational success for Zora. I also discovered that what I'd thought was personal ignorance (*I* didn't know how to teach reading) was actually a national crisis. Parents were far from the only ones missing a clear sense of how reading skills develop and the knowledge needed to nurture them. Teachers, pediatricians, and educational policy makers often lacked this critical insight as well. Most classmates in the Foundations of Reading Instruction course were teachers, and while they knew more than me, they had much to learn, too.

I quickly discovered that being a strong reader scarcely prepares you to teach reading. In fact, many fluent readers aren't consciously aware of the underlying structure of language and print that good teaching must make explicit for children. Teachers, and certainly parents, need to learn to attend to and describe linguistic features that expert readers no longer notice or focus on.

The contrast between (on one hand) abysmal reading performance and (on the other) superficial advice doled out to parents about how to raise readers rankled. Surely the parents who shape a child's reading prospects *for years* before the child enters school should be better informed.

Without any mom-in-the-trenches guidance, I set out to document what I learned about how reading works, the role of parents in fostering it, and what we can (and can't) expect from instruction in schools. I scoured academic literature, reading curricula, state learning standards, government reports, and more. I talked to teachers, tutors, and parents in the thick of raising readers. I served on school, library, and literacy nonprofit boards; volunteered in early-learning programs; and developed databases of research and instructional techniques. I also called top researchers to ask what specific advice they would offer parents today.

My personal effort to better understand what it takes to raise a reader tipped into a larger mission to help all parents learn what's needed to do this vital work.

Why You Need an Action Plan for Your Family

For this book, I've traced the path to literacy from birth through early elementary school with stories and science that illuminate the ways we can influence our kids' success. I hope to give you clear guidance on what to do, when, how, and why.

You may be thinking that plenty of parents set their kids up for educational and career success without deep planning. That they bought picture books, read to kids nightly, enrolled them in good schools, and voilà! But the fact is, a more expansive approach is both possible and invaluable today because of the increasing demands of modern work, school, and life. Your aim isn't to do what proved sufficient for some in previous generations, but rather to do what's likely to prepare your children to reach their full potential.

We'd be foolish to take a back seat, given the indisputable evidence of our power to launch a child's literacy. Research shows, for example, that the number of turn-taking interactions toddlers had in conversations with adults predicted their IQ and language skills *ten years later* as middle schoolers.

And let's be honest, parents across the income and privilege spectrums need that reminder. With increasing demands on our time and growing distractions, such as our ever-alluring smartphones and diminishing work-family boundaries, we have the potential to be less engaged and responsive than we might otherwise.

What parents can accomplish easily early on, through nurturing and natural conversation, may require hard, time-consuming, expensive remediation to catch up on later. Kids need a base level of language proficiency entering kindergarten to fully benefit from classroom instruction. Kindergarten language skills are the single best predictor of school achievement across all subjects in third and fifth grade. And longitudinal research has found evidence that kids who don't read proficiently by third grade are four times as likely to drop out of school.

Studies of the effectiveness of federally funded programs aimed at improving reading skills in adolescents show that they usually had no effect on reading achievement and sometimes even produced negative ones. Even with interventions that appear to be effective, it's hard to determine the size of gains, and it's unclear if any "statistically significant" improvements that resulted are of *practical* significance—that is, strong enough to boost school performance, job prospects, and overall health and well-being. There's a big difference between a program being better than nothing and being good enough for our kids. And programs with negative outcomes are worse than nothing.

Every child deserves full literacy to thrive, and instilling the strongest possible base prior to school gives a child a real shot at gaining the skills and knowledge they'll need long term. Only time can reveal the costs of being unable to rise to the ever-higher levels of reading and writing required to navigate our global, tech-driven society.

When I was growing up, my dad always told me to front-load my effort. He said, "Work as hard as you can to learn as much as you can as fast as you can." That way, when inevitable distractions and unforeseen circumstances arrived, I'd have some wiggle room. Starting strong creates a chance at recovering from setbacks. So it goes with your child's literacy: you will never find a better time than now to launch a reader.

What You'll Get in This Book

The road to reading is long and winding. From diving into the research, talking to parents about their pain points and frustrations, and raising my own reader, I've learned what parents need: a map, some fuel, a maintenance plan, and occasional roadside assistance. You wouldn't embark on any other trip of a lifetime without preparing, would you?

The Lay of the Land

Parents need a big-picture understanding of what reading is, its prerequisite and constituent skills, and a clear picture of what to focus on at each age and stage in their child's development. Without a 10,000-foot view of how reading unfolds from infancy to early elementary school, parents can get stuck spinning their wheels on activities that don't meaningfully support their children.

This book maps the early-learning landscape—the skills, resources, and partners we all need. I'll walk you through the critical early-literacy skills and illustrate how they develop: when to start cultivating them, what mastery looks like, and the milestones in between. I'll give you a framework for understanding how your work as a parent intersects with numerous other players, from pediatricians and librarians to teachers and tutors. I'll also introduce you to leading researchers who will explain their latest findings and make recommendations for how any parent can put these insights to use. This road map will guide your journey and show you how to identify and engage with the advice, materials, information, people, policies, and institutions you're likely to encounter.

Premium Fuel

Parents are often said to be kids' first and best teachers. The "first" part is guaranteed, but the "best" part must be earned. When it comes to literacy, evidence (not intuition) is the best way to judge what works.

Literacy is one of the most-studied topics in academia. There were already more than 100,000 studies on how children learn to read in 1999 when Congress convened the National Reading Panel, and the number has continued to climb. A search for the phrase "reading development" in the National Library of Medicine's biomedical database finds more than 2,500 papers published in 2021 alone. Conferences, publications, and whole careers are devoted to bridging the divide between what research in linguistics, psychology, cognitive science, and education tells us about how reading develops and the practical matter of sparking and accelerating those developments in children.

When parents engage with good research and allow it to inform our decisions and behavior, we benefit from the wisdom of evidence and analysis that's far more revealing than our individual experience or perspective alone. Recent discoveries in neuroscience, molecular biology, and epigenetics alongside years of behavioral and social sciences insights can also boost our empathy by giving us deeper insight into the child's environment and experience. I know I always feel better about my decisions as a mom when they marry responsiveness with effectiveness. I want to do not only what feels right, but also what works.

Routine Maintenance

Becoming literate is considerable work for a child's growing brain, but nurturing it doesn't have to be. Beginning in infancy, parents can foster literacy with warmth, responsiveness, dialogue, and turn-taking. Over time these practices can become core habits and make a lasting impact. In this book, I'll provide simple, everyday strategies to help you find the perspective and build the muscle needed to relate to your children with intention, consistency, and generosity over the long haul.

The fact is, once parents know what the research says about what kids need (and when), there's the practical matter of doing those things day in and day out . . . for years. For that, we need parent-tested and -approved techniques that are easy to fit into busy lives. Putting the time and energy into establishing strong practices early on can rev up lifelong benefits and prevent costly breakdowns.

I'm reminded of an ad I once saw for a project-management system. *Stop using the wrong tool*, it declared, before showing people sawing a piece of paper, eating soup with a fork, opening a can with a wrench, polishing nails with a paint roller, and cleaning eyeglasses with a scrub brush. We need to choose the right tools and then use them in the right ways.

Roadside Assistance

A lot of parenting media treats families as islands. *Read this and teach that*, the books advise, *and your child will learn*. But in reality, reading develops within a dynamic web of relationships and experiences.

Parents need ongoing support from community members, including friends, family, neighbors, teachers, librarians, and others, to keep their kids on track. There's often also a role for the just-in-time intervention of specialists, from speech and hearing therapists to learning and reading experts, depending on a child's particular needs. This is the equivalent of roadside assistance.

Whether you choose to take full responsibility for teaching your child reading or opt to let teachers, tutors, or others do the heavy lifting, subsequent chapters will touch on the most important early considerations—and connections.

———

In his book *Raising Kids Who Read*, cognitive scientist Daniel Willingham warns parents to "resist the urge to engage in reading instruction unless you have reason to believe you know what you're doing." He's got a point. I'm calling on all parents to accept the challenge to *learn* what you're doing and *teach* what you can. Your child's education just might depend on it.

Are you ready to get started? The following pages provide a family reading road map, fuel for your journey, a tune-up checklist, and roadside support for when you feel adrift or need a jump-start. Let's go!

1

Beyond Bedtime Stories: The Truth about Getting Kids Ready to Read

Keep in mind always the present you are constructing. It should be the future you want.

—Alice Walker

A mom-friend and I had been having a forgettable chat in a picturesque little café when I brought it up. A subject that made her visibly tense.

I'd known her as an unflappable, high-powered management consultant turned tech executive. She was a visionary always spoiling for a challenge worthy of her considerable skills and talents. Thoughtful and strategic, she brought a commanding yet optimistic presence to meetings and made people want to rise to the heights of her ambitious proposals.

But on that day, I struck a nerve with an offhand remark about how little parents know about teaching their kids to read, that is, how we're just told to read to them every day and wait for the magic to set in.

"I used to get so angry when I would hear that advice," she said. "I was working so hard when my kids were little. I didn't have an hour to read to them every night and I felt so bad about it." She re-called hoping at the time that enrolling the kids in "good schools" would make up for the storytime deficit. Still, she had carried guilt about it for years. Her kids were in high school by the time I met her, but the memory pained her. She may have given her kids her all, but in her mind, she'd come up short on that one measure and didn't let herself forget it.

I've been a part of countless conversations about raising readers, and they tend to get emotional. I've heard the heartfelt testimony of a woman who records incarcerated mothers reading picture books and then ships the books and recordings to their kids, so they can have some semblance of a bedtime ritual with Mom. I've heard from multilingual parents who fret about passing on their first language without undermining their child's progress learning English. I've spoken with parents after they've just received the jarring news of a child's dyslexia diagnosis. They all grappled with intense feelings of worry and frustration that come from discovering their children had a need they didn't know how to meet. You can hear the edge of panic in their tones.

The café conversation stuck with me, though, because this parent's angst wasn't coming from an obviously vulnerable space. The family wasn't in crisis. Her kids had performed well in school and were on the cusp of launching into college. Theirs was an educational success story, judged by most standards but her own.

Around the same time, I spoke with another mom who said she *had* made time to read to her three sons at length every night for more than a decade. Yet she was just as tortured by her decision to go all-in as the mom who hadn't. The second mom had clung to the bedtime ritual like a badge of honor, but her middle son still struggled with reading. He lacked the skill and motivation to read well for himself and had recently bombed his state achievement test.

"But I read to him every night," she told me, expressing her sense that she'd been cheated out of an expected return. She was angry that she'd have to pay a tutor to teach what he'd missed, that she hadn't acted earlier on signs that he needed more support, that what worked for one child didn't work for all. "I noticed he read like a robot, but thought it just takes some kids longer."

How could it be that moms at both ends of the spectrum—one who had read every night and one who hadn't—both described nearly identical feelings of inadequacy, uncertainty, and disappointment? The answer, I came to understand, was in the singular focus on bedtime reading. Both clung to the particular raise-a-reader tactic as *the* measure of their influence. And both suffered for it. That's because our loud cultural push for daily reading aloud, devoid of proper context, has a way of both shaming those who can't instill the habit and giving a false sense of security to those who can.

Both moms had fixated on a storytime-to-success message that resounds in the press, libraries, schools, and parenting programs. The well-intended advice is everywhere, but its delivery tends to raise more questions than it answers. Like most fairy tales, this particular story is well-worn, fractured with each retelling, and prone to magical leaps. It skips over crucial detail about the long, winding, and often plodding roads to reading. Day-to-day life with little kids exposes the missing plot points: How do you make family reading a habit? And if you do, does the ritual really bring about the host of benefits it's been praised for? What else is required of parents to get the job done?

A magazine warns, "Young kids whose parents read them five books a day enter kindergarten having heard 1.4 million more words than kids who aren't read to . . . and one's kindergarten vocabulary predicts future academic success." Real-world parents wonder how short those five books may be, and how fast those parents read.

A grocery chain's book drive reminds shoppers that "the single most significant factor influencing a child's early educational success is an introduction to books and being read to at home prior to beginning school." The pressure's on, and shoppers with toddlers in tow worry about what exactly qualifies as "an introduction" and how far before kindergarten we're talking.

An author declares, "The rewards of early reading are astonishingly meaningful: toddlers who have lots of stories read to them turn into children who are more likely to enjoy strong relationships, sharper focus, and greater emotional resilience and self-mastery. The evidence has become so overwhelming that social scientists now consider read-aloud time one of the most important indicators of a child's prospects in life." Our antennae go up. *Bedtime stories do all that?*

We get the message: reading aloud is a multivitamin for kids and a proxy for good parenting, too. If you do it each night, you can build their brains and inspire a lifetime of literary delight, family bonding, and accomplishment.

Of course, there's more to the story. Reading aloud, though valuable, isn't everything. It's time to move beyond fairy tales and to root your own reading story in reality.

The Top Six Parent Levers for Literacy

When it comes to getting kids off to a strong start, parents are in the driver's seat, but it's like one of those dual-control driving-school cars with two steering wheels, accelerators, and brakes—one set for the student and one for the instructor. Even babies who haven't spoken a word are actively learning and growing. You're not pouring information into an empty vessel. You're responding to your child's gaze, gestures, vocalizations, and (eventually) words, and stimulating more.

A time will come when you hand over the keys, take a back seat, or exit the car altogether. But initially, you're in it together, and you've got a great deal of learning to do yourself about how to encourage, teach, and advocate for your child. You know how to drive, but you've still got to get familiar with all the buttons and levers to help your child do the same. You've also got to keep scanning the horizon to see how their current language environment and experiences will impact future success—insights that are possible thanks to advances in experimental studies, brain imaging, and more. With this vision in place, you'll be better equipped to nurture their literacy, years before they can be expected to distinguish letters or sounds, let alone read words or paragraphs.

As pediatric surgeon and early-language advocate Dana Suskind writes, "Without a concerted look, we might actually believe that the problems we see in older children start at the moment we observe them." In fact, research shows vast cognitive function disparities between infants as young as 9 months old, and sizable vocabulary and wide real-time language processing gaps are evident among toddlers.

There are countless ways that a parent can make a difference early on, but the following six are the most powerful to leverage as infants and toddlers grow into preschoolers and kindergarteners. I introduce them here and then revisit them in depth in Chapters 5 through 9, so you have several sample practices, talking points, and tips to test-drive for yourself.

Lever #1: Conversation

Early talk is our point of greatest leverage for improving children's futures.

—LENA

Want your child's IQ and academic performance to land off the charts? Then launch their learning and language development with lots of conversation when they're young. I can't reiterate this finding enough: kids who engage in more back-and-forth dialogue with adults when they're 18 to 24 months old tend to have a significantly higher IQ and better language skills as adolescents than kids who lack frequent back-and-forth adult-child conversations. Simply put, conversation spurs brain development.

LENA, a national nonprofit focused on enhancing early-language experiences, has collected recordings of thousands of children, families, and caregivers talking in their natural environments (at home or at childcare), not in laboratories. Analysis of those daylong recordings reveals that the *dynamism* of the conversation—how much the child participates and responds—matters, not merely the number of words spoken to or by them.

The data showed that talkative toddlers with talkative parents grew into middle schoolers with better reasoning, logic, problem-solving abilities, verbal comprehension, and vocabulary skills than kids who had experienced fewer "conversational turns" during the pivotal time frame.

Research by a team at Harvard University, MIT, and the University of Pennsylvania gives some insight into *how* verbal exchanges work their brain-magic to boost language skills, cognitive capacity, and academic achievement down the road. Using functional MRI technology, researchers found that the more conversational turns children had experienced with adults, the greater the activity in their Broca's area (a region associated with speech production and language processing) during a story-listening task. In the duet of conversation, the level of responsiveness to a kid's speech seems to affect language processing in their brains. In another study by some of the same researchers, diffusion MRI revealed that conversational turns change the *physical structure* of the brain by forging stronger links between Broca's area and Wernicke's area (a region associated with speech comprehension).

For parents, these peeks into brain function and structure expose some roots of the variations we see in language development. They also suggest strategies for getting kids off to a strong start, which later chapters describe. Nurture your child's linguistic development from day one by exchanging words, gestures, and expressions with them. (Easier said than done in the age of the smartphone, when text messages, social media, and electronic notifications drive parents to chronic distraction.) Your effort and attention will show up in their IQ, listening comprehension, and vocabulary scores when they are teens.

Although this book emphasizes the importance of oral language for reading development, I want to note that the path to reading is different for deaf and hard-of-hearing people who lack full access to the sounds of spoken language. For deaf children, overall language ability is a stronger predictor of reading skill. American Sign Language, which has its own syntax and grammar, unrelated to those of English, is the primary language of many deaf and hard-of-hearing children. And early access to sign language seems to help literacy development. Skilled deaf signers are often better readers than deaf individuals who are not proficient in sign language.

When I brought my daughter home from the hospital, I was in survival mode, consumed with worry about car seat safety and breast milk supply. I needed to get her home and keep her fed. A few days in, more confident in the bare essentials, I started reading to her. But no one told me the specifics of how to talk to her or the urgency of why. I didn't grasp my full power to build her brain and boost her emergent communication skills through words and responsiveness. In fact, 94 percent of moms in one study said that no health professional had ever talked with them about their newborn's language development. The doctors, nurses, and pediatricians who advise us often focus on immediate matters of safety. Now I know that early-childhood language affects life prospects, too.

In Chapter 6, we'll explore early-language research, plus the simplest, proven ways to implement its recommendations. We all bring different cultural, familial, and individual preferences to how (and how much) we talk, but most of us could stand to converse much more with our kids. Hang on to this insight and you're well on your way to speaking up when kids need your words, warmth, and responsiveness most. Even on the busiest, most exhausting, distracting, and turbulent days, this urgent truth can help you find your voice.

Lever #2: Book Reading

Books are meat and medicine
and flame and flight and flower,
steel, stitch, and cloud and clout,
and drumbeats in the air.

—Gwendolyn Brooks

Reading out loud didn't get a reputation as "the single most important activity for helping children become literate" for nothing. It *is* pivotal for boosting brain capacity, stimulating language development, spurring vocabulary growth, increasing knowledge about the world, driving kids' motivation to read on their own, and more. It's just not the be-all, end-all. Parents need to know that there's more to raising a reader than reading aloud *and* that there's more to reading aloud than reciting words on the page.

Children have so much to learn in the first years of life, and book reading is one powerful strategy to support development as their needs change. Newborns developing their vision may prefer to look at high-contrast images like those in black-and-white board books. Meanwhile, 6-to-12-month-olds get their eyes, hands, feet, and mouths in on the action by engaging with different page features, like textures and flaps. Toddlers are busy building their vocabularies and love simple books full of familiar items, plus a healthy dose of rhythm, rhyme, and repetition.

And so it goes for years. The benefits of reading aloud shift with the child's age, needs, interests, and the nature of the texts. Over time, family reading introduces more complex and novel words than typical everyday speech, facilitates focus on and learning about print and spelling (as opposed to just spoken language), and delivers fodder for greater comprehension, to name a few benefits. Reading together is so effective because it creates more opportunities for the kind of rich conversation described in Lever #1.

The page provides story, eye candy, and language. The parent brings experience, speech, and enthusiasm. The child engages with the book and with their parent's voice and offers attention and language of their own. The three parties—book, parent, and child—commune differently every time. Even rereadings of familiar texts are novel, because our demeanor and attention changes from moment to moment, from day to day.

Studies show that a literature-rich home environment, exemplified by having a large home library or routine engagement with books, bolsters kids' grades and standardized test performance. One analysis found that a robust home library in childhood was associated with better literacy, numeracy, and technological problem-solving skills well into adulthood—beyond the benefits that come from parents' education or career accomplishments. And those long-lasting advantages held across pooled data from more than two dozen societies spanning four continents.

As the researchers put it, "In sum, the benefits of bookishness for attainment are beyond question . . . Early exposure to books in parental home matters because books are an integral part of routines and practices which enhance life-long cognitive competencies."

Like the 9-month-old who is figuring out how to recognize faces, respond to sounds with sounds, and pass things from hand to hand, you too have a lot to learn. You'll tap into the full teaching potential of literature when you use resources like this guide to understand what's happening with your child developmentally. With that knowledge, you'll be better able to select engaging books and to supplement the text with the comments and questions likely to maximize learning. Chapter 2 overviews the road to reading age by age and offers suggestions for what to read when. Making researching, observing, and responding a habit will help you find the right titles to impart the lessons your child needs in each stage.

That's parent power.

Lever #3: Teaching

Just as war is "too serious a matter to be left to the generals," so, I think, the teaching of reading is too important to be left to the educators.

—Rudolf Flesch

Parents need to teach reading, not just model it, because (unlike with spoken language) most kids don't learn to read well without intentional, direct instruction—which many schools are ill-equipped to deliver, especially when kids arrive without solid preparation. Witness the skyrocketing demand for private tutoring in the elementary years and the low reading-achievement scores among demographics that can't access supplemental instruction. That said, home instruction needn't imitate the classroom approach. The style that I recommend is more gradual and integrated than typical school instruction.

A big mistake parents make is separating skills from meaningful, motivating, thought-provoking context. When confronting the vastness and complexity of reading skills, you may want to simplify your work by hammering away at some tiny part of the whole. You know kids need to know their letters, so you drill them. You know they have to learn words, so you get a list for them to stare at and (you hope) memorize. A better approach would be to give them multifaceted experience with a word's spelling, pronunciation, and meaning. It takes knowledge of all three (preferably in contexts kids care about, like conversation, books they're reading, even shows they are watching) to make a word stick in memory.

Caregivers have different opportunities and need different strategies than classroom teachers because we're operating in the wilds of our homes and daily lives, not in a setting marked by bells and boundaries. Effectiveness comes with matching the lesson to the child and the moment. Depending on their age, stage, and interests, you could be teaching through song or play, reading or writing, or talking and listening.

What spurs learning is your clarity around what you're trying to impart (alphabetic knowledge, sound awareness, vocabulary) and your thoughtful selection of a method (play, nursery rhymes, conversation). It's having the knowledge to teach what you intend for kids to learn that makes a difference.

Take, for example, thinking out loud and explaining yourself. These are powerful and underappreciated teaching methods that parents have available to us, because they give kids insights into the invisible dimensions of reading. The old three-part public speaking advice—*tell 'em what you're going to tell 'em, tell 'em, and then tell 'em what you told 'em*—applies here.

When teaching, give kids a preview of the insight you're about to share, so they know what to look and listen for, talk out your thought process step by step, and then sum up your point. Bonus points if you give the child an opportunity to give it a try themselves to cement the learning.

For example, if you're trying to bring your child's attention to the sounds within a word, you could model the behavior by saying the word with exaggerated emphasis on the sounds within it and hope they intuit what you did. But a better approach would be to frame the lesson: set it up, break it down, and prompt them to practice. You could say, *I'm going to say a word with three sounds inside it. Listen and see if you can hear the sounds.* Mat *I hear /m/, /a/, /t/. What sounds do you hear in* cat? *Yes, /k/, /a/, /t/. Now you say a word and tell me what sounds you hear inside it.*

There are countless straightforward but powerful literacy lessons like these that parents can deliver when *we* are shown how. Don't worry. You'll find ample guidance in this book on how to seize everyday teachable moments. Chapters 5 through 9 show integrated approaches to easily teaching the reading skills that matter most.

Lever #4: Connecting

*Some people think they are in community, but they are only in
proximity. True community requires commitment and openness.
It is a willingness to extend yourself to encounter and know the
other.*

—David Spangler

Roads to reading are personal. As a parent in the thick of leveraging
resources for your child's benefit, you will often cross paths with
others who may alter your course. They may share an idea, information, or invitation of significance. They may spark your child's interest or skills in unexpected ways, or step up to support you when
your time, energy, or resources flag.

Consequently, part of the work you'll do to support your child
will be intentionally cultivating relationships with people who have
the insights and access your family needs. Here are some people
who may aid your family's reading journey:

TEACHERS. Hopefully, your child's teachers will facilitate vital
literacy skills. But they can be just as valuable in identifying issues
that require additional support and directing you to other professionals who can better meet your particular child's needs. I'm reminded of a report I read about one mom who was advocating for
better support services for her son. She found a tremendous ally in
his teacher, who went side by side with her all the way to the level of
a school-district hearing.

But more often I've witnessed cases where parents took offense
when teachers said they couldn't fully support a particular child in
class. So hear this: when a teacher tells you it's time to call in rein-
forcements, believe them. The limits of their resources, time, and

training are real. Don't get mad; get busy finding the right person or people to meet the need.

LIBRARIANS. A good children's librarian can help you find your next favorite read, but that's not all. Thanks to initiatives like Every Child Ready to Read, created by the Public Library Association and the Association for Library Service to Children, librarians are becoming parent educators as well. There's growing awareness among librarians that families need support in cultivating key early-literacy skills through talking, reading, writing, singing, and playing. They are responding by showing parents how to make the most of story-time through asking questions and engaging kids in dialogue and play around stories. Recognize libraries and librarians themselves as resources beyond the books on their shelves, and you may access a range of learning experiences for your child and activity ideas for yourself.

DOCTORS. Medical professionals can be excellent resources for monitoring your child's progress toward developmental milestones, providing referrals to speech, hearing, and other specialists if needed. Increasingly, they are also direct providers of books for kids and reading guidance for parents, thanks to the American Academy of Pediatrics' emphasis on early-literacy promotion as a tenet of care.

More and more doctors are taking this role to heart. Dr. Robin Foster, then chief of pediatric emergency services at VCU Medical Center in Richmond, Virginia, took the concept to the emergency room as well. She and nurses in her department brought Reach Out and Read, a national program that integrates children's books and parental advice into medical visits, to kids who visited the ER. Many families were repeat visitors, because of either complex medical situations or lack of insurance, and Foster said that she made as much impact on these vulnerable families through social engagement like the books program as she did with medical intervention.

OTHER PARENTS. Moms of older children can be invaluable sources of information. They have the latest intel on the best teachers, what kinds of challenges kids faced as they moved from grade to grade, and how to find the good summer camps and enrichment programs.

Cultivating fruitful relationships with peers and experts is easy: inquire about their work and interests, dig into the materials and info they recommend or produce, share relevant resources with them, ask meaningful questions. Repeat.

Lever #5: Budgeting

Don't tell me where your priorities are. Show me where you spend your money and I'll tell you what they are.

—James Frick

Money talks. Or, in this case, money can pay people to talk with, assess, read to, teach, and support your child. I've never seen *spending* listed in a magazine roundup of ways parents can boost reading achievement, but it is. I think it's important to say so, plainly, to parents of young children, so that they understand it's among their options when they can't meet all their child's learning needs on their own. And what parent can?

When my daughter was entering elementary school and I spoke with parents of older children about their school experiences, I was shocked by how commonplace tutoring was. One friend paid her son's teacher to tutor him over the summer, to repeat reading lessons that hadn't taken hold during the school year. Another took out a high-interest loan to cover out-of-school reading support with a national learning center.

The big supplementary educational spending wasn't limited to my high-earning, high-achieving neighbors. In the decades since many of us were kids, there's been a steady rise in tutoring for young children—even preschoolers. In fact, some observers date the first "explosion in demand" for preschool tutoring to 2002 and 2003. That means we're entering a time when millennials who themselves were tutored as preschoolers are becoming parents.

Industry analysts expect preschool tutoring enrollment, which has grown over the last five years, to continue to boom at least through 2026 as disposable income rebounds from the pandemic. All this tells us that tutoring kids before elementary school is not new, it's not limited to an overexuberant fringe of parents, and it's not going anywhere soon.

Most often, today's parents are spending on tutoring out of real concern for getting their kids ready for kindergarten or on "grade level" once they're school-aged. Plus, cohorts of young children whose early childcare and education were affected by the COVID-19 pandemic will need extra supports, tutoring or otherwise, over time as well.

Should parents have to pay to secure basic literacy skills for their kids? No. Do they? Often, yes. Private tutoring is a major, long-standing player in American education with implications for how, when, and whether kids fulfill their reading potential. But it's not the only one.

Literacy spending may deserve a place among the priorities you weigh when budgeting your family's resources, alongside saving, healthcare, vacations, and so on. Beyond tutoring, financial investment in learning evaluations, educational experiences, private schools, and high-quality childcare are all major factors driving better literacy outcomes for many. And don't discount smaller, everyday purchases like books, field trips, and after-school activities. They also contribute to the richness of kids' vocabulary, background knowledge, and enthusiasm for learning.

Many parents make up for what they lack in money with creativity in engineering the experiences and access their child needs, meticulously tracking free-admission days at local cultural institutions and borrowing or making supplies they can't buy. Sometimes it comes down to choices like paying for a visit to a science museum versus a sports match, an enrichment class versus an amusement park. Conscious spending means recognizing the trade-offs we make every day and considering their impact.

This book focuses on free and inexpensive ways to nurture reading, and I'm a huge fan of the free books and programming that libraries provide. Still, it's important to note that how parents deploy the money they have makes an impact: spending to provide more of the language, experiences, and instruction kids need is an option.

Lever #6: Advocacy

Look at the world around you. It may seem like an immovable, implacable place. It is not. With the slightest push—in just the right place—it can be tipped.

—Malcolm Gladwell

When kids enter school or childcare, it becomes more obvious that our role as parents includes overseeing how well *other* people and institutions meet their needs. But raising a reader is a collaborative project from the outset. From the pediatrician we ask about developmental progress to librarians running programs we attend, we need others to nurture their learning alongside us.

Sometimes we can just request help and seek out resources, but sometimes we must push beyond that into advocacy—encouraging better support, funding, accountability, and equity for ourselves, our kids, and the broader community of children. This isn't necessarily about lobbying Congress. Advocacy comes in many forms and might look like sharing information with your child's school or teacher about the crucial importance of back-and-forth talk, monitoring the classroom video feed for evidence that the point was taken, and then scheduling a meeting if meaningful verbal engagement with the kids doesn't occur.

Some parents worry about being too pushy, and it's true that you don't want to alienate teachers with excessive demands or hover to the point of shielding your child from everyday adversity. But there's a big difference between those extremes and engaging in healthy dialogue about beneficial practices for your child and their peers. The kind of advocacy I'm talking about serves to bolster the quality of education all kids in the school or classroom are likely to receive.

This may seem uncomfortable, even extreme, but good early-childcare and education programs want engaged parents. They invite families to participate, encourage two-way communication, and welcome information about your child's particular needs and circumstances. Close family-school connections are so critical that they top the National Association for the Education of Young Children (NAEYC) list of principles of effective family engagement. Specifically, NAEYC recommends that families and teachers jointly set educational goals and that families actively participate in the school community.

In fact, many parents overlook meaningful opportunities to get

involved that come their way via school, childcare, and neighborhood communications. The newsletter blurb seeking volunteers for
the parent advisory council presents a chance to learn about how a
school works and how to effect change. The pamphlet offering facil-
ities tours gives insight into the learning spaces your child will navigate and the occasion to ask questions about instructional needs
and priorities. The strategic planning survey about the future of
schools in your community invites your voice and participation,
too. So, take your chances to get involved—in a thoughtful, positive way.

To return to the preceding back-and-forth talk example, a parent
could ask childcare administrators to provide staff training that covers early-childhood brain development and the power of talk. They
could volunteer for organizations that provide such training, make
donations to those groups, or lobby for professional development
resources. They could offer to fund-raise to cover the costs of more
training or apply for grants on behalf of the center. They could even
dig into the larger policies and government funding that make high-
quality care accessible or inaccessible in the first place.

The advocacy possibilities are endless (including urging better
support for kids who aren't struggling), but it all starts with opening
our eyes, ears, and mouths to discern our kids' particular needs and
ensuring that they're met. We must get comfortable observing and
asking questions to help us better understand reading development,
recognize where our children are, and grasp what they need to foster
future growth. Whoever you are and whatever your experience with
school policy and curriculum, remember that your job is to bring
deep care and concern for your child and all children into discussions with teachers and school officials.

You don't have to have all the answers; you just need to continue asking questions until you understand. If you don't feel confident in raising questions or taking action, seek out family members, friends, or community members who can help you. Many cities even have organizations focused on building a healthy education ecosystem, including programs that train parents to push for positive change. For example, the Family Leadership Institute in Milwaukee hosts six-week learning experiences to teach parents about local school issues and how to use community-organizing principles to address them.

Anyone can advocate for children, including people who don't have any or whose kids are grown, but as a parent of a young child, you bring special perspective and deep experience that can inspire and inform others to act as well. In many ways, advocacy is the culmination of the parent levers described earlier. When you do your best to cultivate your child's literacy, you will feel the limits of your efforts and have a sharper vision for what needs to change—at home, in schools, and in the community—for your child and all children to thrive.

Try This at Home
Journal the Journey

Power and *influence* aren't the terms most frequently associated with parenthood or early literacy. But I think they should be, because parents are difference makers in seeding critical reading skills from day one and, as this chapter illustrates, we have a range of levers at our disposal to do that.

To fulfill your potential as your child's first teacher and best advocate, it helps to do something that teachers and advocates do—designate time and space to think and plan. Start a for-your-eyes-only journal to take note of what you've learned, what you're doing well and should continue, what needs tweaking or eliminating, and what else you'd like to investigate or try.

I'll provide prompts at the end of each chapter to point you toward things to reflect on, note, or observe along your family reading journey. If you're reading this before your child is born or while they are in infancy, just skip questions that don't apply. You can revisit and journal about them when your child grows older.

Keep the journal on your nightstand or another visible location as a reminder to write out your thoughts, ideas, discoveries, and questions. This cumulative notetaking and reflection will be invaluable for helping you discover your strengths as a conversation partner, reader, teacher, advocate, and more. When you know where you excel, you can more consciously bring those strengths to supporting your child's development.

JOURNAL PROMPTS

- What role do you want to play in nurturing and teaching your child to read?

- What strengths and experiences do you bring to the role?

- Do you have questions or concerns about your knowledge or ability to support reading development?

- What can you do today to nurture reading skills? What can you do today to nurture reading love? What overlap do you see between reading skills and reading love?

2

The Long Run: How to Nurture
Reading at Each Age and Stage

There are years that ask questions and years that answer.
—Zora Neale Hurston

Now that you've been introduced to the key tools available to parents, it's time to explore the road to reading from the child's perspective, from infancy through early elementary school. Remember that dual-driver car? The best instructors are attuned to what the student sees and understands, so that they can patiently usher them toward greater skill and knowledge.

Let's start by setting realistic expectations. Your baby cannot read. It's not even something you should aspire to, let alone try to teach, despite the bogus claims of some products and the wishful thinking of the parents who buy them. The path to reading unfolds over the course of years, not months, and trying to shortcut the process can misdirect you from providing the critical early support and guidance that are shown to predict later reading achievement and school success.

Reading is making sense of print at a glance. It's accessing the sound of words from letters and grasping words' meanings, too—the people, places, things, and concepts they are meant to represent. There's no evidence that babies can do that. At. All.

The parents' job in the beginning is not to teach reading but to nurture its long-term development through active attention, book sharing, and caring conversation. Think of these as your own ABCs. Do them thoughtfully and consistently from the start, and you will create a rich early-language environment in which your child's reading can bloom. No flash cards, computer screens, or baby "curriculum" required.

In this chapter, you'll find a chronology of language and literacy milestones to help you anticipate the vocabulary, alphabetic knowledge, and sound awareness that your child should accumulate as they grow. By the end of this quick tour, you'll better understand how your action ABCs (attention, book sharing, conversation) in the early years fuel your child's growth from cooer and babbler to full-fledged reader and communicator.

Although origin details are hotly contested, many linguists believe that modern human speech abilities, including the production of contrasting vowel sounds, may have emerged millions of years ago. That span has given the modern human brain ample time to evolve the wiring that enables even very young children to produce and understand speech in their native language with ease. Today, children's oral-language development is thought to proceed along a straightforward and predictable path with observable milestones (e.g., first coos, babbles, and spoken words). In this chapter, I will list some developmental markers that align with norms published by organizations including the American Speech-Language-Hearing Association, the National Institute on Deafness and Other Communication Disorders, and the Centers for Disease Control. The time frames I list correspond roughly to when most monolingual children will reach the milestones, according to analysis of parent surveys and other research.

I'll also list selected milestones related to reading skills. The ability to read a written language, in contrast to the ability to speak a language, doesn't emerge effortlessly. Rather, it's a complex learned ability that emerged much more recently in human history with the advent of writing systems. Researchers have proposed that it requires the "recycling" of brain networks that originally evolved for other purposes. To read, kids must have the requisite oral-language foundation, plus accumulate sufficient instruction and experience with *written* language to grasp the alphabetic principle that letters in print relate to sounds in speech. There's incredible variation in how long it takes people to become skilled readers—and far too many never get there. For this reason, the time frames I give for written language "milestones" are more accurately called *targets*. That is, they represent when peer-reviewed research suggests kids would benefit from having certain skills and knowledge in order to meet grade-level expectations down the road—not necessarily when most kids actually do achieve these skills.

Keep in mind that your family's mileage *will vary*. The chronology that follows isn't a standardized, validated screening tool nor a curriculum guide. Moreover, it's not meant to trigger a guilt trip about what you did or didn't know or do at any given point in time. If your child is older, scan the list to see all that they've learned or where they might need support. Then read ahead to see what's still coming. Get on board with doing what you can *now* to move forward from where your child is, and to help them learn and accomplish what they need next for school and life.

You can also visit readingforourlives.com/milestones for more in-depth information on the language and literacy signposts described in this chapter, the research underpinning them, and ideas on what to do if you are concerned about your child's development.

May the following lists of milestones remind you of the incredible number of cognitive, motor, language, and literacy skills that kids must acquire—and give you the patience and perspective to be a loving guide.

All Ears in the Third Trimester

Well, we might as well start from the top. There's evidence that initial memory and learning of voices and language begins before birth. By the third trimester of pregnancy, the sound of a mother's voice may be transmitted from the amniotic fluid through the fetus's skull and into the inner ear. So go ahead and speak up. Talk to your baby bump, because research findings indicate that exposure to ambient language in the womb likely contributes to phonetic perception.

Fun fact: there's evidence that experience with vowels affects babies' perception earlier than experience with consonants, because "vowels are louder, longer in duration and carry salient prosodic information (melody, rhythm and stress)." One study of newborns in the United States and Sweden found evidence that newborns distinguished between and reacted differently to vowel sounds from their native (familiar) language and another language. Why? Because they'd been hearing and getting used to vowel sounds from their native language for weeks in the womb.

Picture newborn babies, just 20 hours old, lying on their backs in bassinets with sensor-fitted, computer-connected pacifiers in their mouths and padded headphones next to their ears. That's how the researchers tested their hypothesis!

Crying, Cooing, and Giggling from
Birth to 6 Months

In the beginning, your newborn baby is speechless, except for a symphony of intermittent crying. They use the only sounds they know to tell you how they feel: whines of discomfort, low rumbles of hunger, and the soft moans of fatigue.

Your challenge is to tend to the immediate need—change the diaper, feed the baby, sing the lullaby—while also recognizing crying's place in a broader language, learning, and literacy journey. As children's speech and language therapist Nicola Lathey puts it, "Crying is, in fact, nature's way of enabling a baby to climb the language development ladder!" *Waaaaaah!*—those long vowel sounds are the seeds of words to come.

By the third month of life, infants add coos (comfort sounds in stress-free situations) to the mix, and win caregivers' attention and loving responses. It's easy to overlook the learning happening amid the immediacy of feeding, clothing, and washing that makes up newborn life. But, with practice, you can tune in, and you'll be rewarded with new insights and discoveries. You'll be able to notice the precious moments when cries become more speechlike in tone, as your little one gradually gains more control of their voice.

Beyond verbal communication, there's a lot of language development going on through gestures, facial expressions, and even eye gaze. Infants pay a lot of attention to and learn from what they see, including what they see you looking at. Evidence suggests that babies start following their caregivers' gaze between 2 and 4 months old—and evidence shows that they tend to learn more with gaze cues than without them.

Even though they won't be able to read the words, include books from day one to get yourself into a routine of talking and reading to your baby. By 6 months old, they can enjoy hearing and physically exploring books. Board or vinyl books with limited text and unadorned illustrations provide the right-fit visual and tactile stimulation your infant needs. Books with poems and nursery rhymes, too, regardless of illustrations, make it easy to use your voice in a way that will please little ears.

Start sharing books with your baby and begin discovering what they like best. Every baby is different, and yes, they have preferences. It's fun to see their reactions—reaching for the pages, pushing books away, even falling asleep when uninterested. From the get-go, your baby is driving their own learning by following their interests and gathering information. Isn't that incredible?

Although some books make it easier to support your child where they are now, don't stress about picking the "perfect" first books. There are none. As literacy specialists Caroline J. Blakemore and Barbara Weston Ramirez put it in their book, *Baby Read-Aloud Basics: Fun and Interactive Ways to Help Your Little One Discover the World of Words,* "Your choice of books is not as important as making the choice to read to your baby on a regular basis." So choosing books *you* enjoy is powerful, too.

Judge books by their shortness and sweetness at this age, not their literary merits. You're likely to hold your infant's attention on a book for only a minute or two, so you might as well make it a fun, complete experience by picking a book that delivers language and visual interest fast. And here's a pro tip that Susan Neuman, a professor of childhood and literacy education at New York University, shared with me: "Quit before they get restless. You end at the crest of the wave."

SELECTED BIRTH-TO-6-MONTH MILESTONES

Oral Language

- Cries
- Coos (2–3 months)
- Growls, squeals, blows raspberries, and other forms of vocal play (4–6 months)
- Recognizes and responds to your voice

Book Behavior

- Looks at books
- Grasps books without using thumb
- Sees print and images on pages
- Prefers to look at higher-contrast images and human faces

Babbling Away from 6 to 12 Months

The language-learning journey continues in the latter half of the first year, through back-and-forth exchanges between you and your baby. By this age, babies may respond to simple requests like *Come here*, imitate your speech, and shake their head no. They explore the world around them by gazing at and reaching for things, then passing the objects from hand to hand or hand to mouth.

They're also getting more active in telling you what they think. They make sounds in response to the sounds they hear and to express pleasure or discontentment. They answer to their names, look where you point, and point at things themselves.

And now, believe it or not, is prime time to make read-alouds interactive. One study found evidence that when moms directed more questions to their 10-month-olds while reading stories, their children had better expressive and receptive language skills at 18 months old than children whose mothers had directed fewer questions to them.

(Sorry, no dads were included in this research.) The toddlers who'd been peppered with questions like *What's that? Where's the doggie? Do you wanna turn the pages? Ready?* during storytime as babies showed a greater ability to understand what others said to them. They also showed a higher capacity to communicate their needs, thoughts, and ideas using words, phrases, and gestures. So there's value in reading books and asking related questions, even before kids can answer fully. Through being read to, babies learn language, background knowledge, the concept of print, new words, and more.

How does that sound?

SELECTED 6-TO-12-MONTH MILESTONES
Oral Language
- Babbles with long and short strings of consonant-vowel combinations (e.g., *babababab*)
- Babbles may mirror the rising and falling intonation of caregiver questions
- Uses sounds and gestures to capture your attention
- Turns toward sounds
- Recognizes their own name
- Plays peekaboo and pat-a-cake

Book Behavior
- Grasps books using their thumbs
- Pats, strokes, scratches books
- Uses feet or mouth to touch books
- Sees as well as adults
- Directs their eye gaze to large, bright, and/or high-contrast pictures in books
- Points to pictures in books

Making Words and Posing Questions
from 12 to 24 Months

Susie Allison, creator of the popular busytoddler Instagram account, thinks some kids in this age range need their own title, since they're no longer babies, but not quite toddlers, either. She proposes *taby* (to rhyme with *baby*) as the name for this group that has "all the ideas of a toddler but none of the motor skills to make it happen."

Indeed, these kiddos are stacking blocks, pouring sand and water, nesting cups, and hustling to combine a lot of different skills. Meantime, they're grasping for the words they need to express themselves, too. One year in and children are beginning to speak: *mama*, *dada*, *uh-oh*, and the like. After 18 months, their spoken vocabulary takes off, as they're often talking like crazy and learning several new words a day.

Whatever their vocabulary size, keep treating and responding to any speechlike (non-cry, non-digestive) sounds coming from your child as genuine talk. Respond within five seconds, and (as noted in Chapter 1) there's evidence that those "conversational turns" may help bolster your little one's brain connectivity and brain function now, as well as their language skills and IQ scores down the road (also as noted in Chapter 1).

Gestures come into play in a bigger way now, too. One-year-olds are already doing some pretty sophisticated coordination of their sounds, gestures, and eye gaze to get your attention. One study found that when infants coordinate their gaze to a caregiver's face while gesturing or vocalizing, the caregivers were more likely to respond. The frequency of infants' gaze-coordinated vocalizations that a caregiver gave a timely response to was the best predictor of expressive vocabulary development up to 2 years old. When babies' vocalizations were rewarded with a response, they learned to express themselves better.

Your little one may even start following your directions to pick up toys or point to an object they want. They may make sense of longer questions from you: *Where are Daddy's keys?* They'll also start asking parents a lot of questions, too: *What's that?*

All of this early speech and vocabulary learning is critical for later reading, because for an emergent reader to make sense of a word in print, they need to have heard it before. (Or, usually, many times before.) Selecting books that reflect daily life deepen the learning at this age. Little narratives about kids playing, putting on clothes, or having breakfast may pique your toddler's interest. And some children's authors also take care to make first-word books that are entertaining for parents, too, by building in as much humor and suspense as a board book can handle. You can even make your own books featuring pictures of friends, family, and familiar places. That's personal relevance in teaching at its best.

SELECTED 12-TO-24-MONTH MILESTONES
Oral Language and Gestures
- Says single words or repeated syllables
- Uses *I* and *it* pronouns
- Points to named objects in books
- Shakes head to indicate *yes* and *no*
- Lifts arms to signal *pick me up* or *hand me that*
- Gestures increase in quantity and complexity

Book Behavior and Writing
- Handles standard books
- Turns pages in books
- Enjoys being read to
- Recognizes familiar books' covers

- Points to and names familiar characters and objects in books
- Points to things they want you to name
- Holds and makes marks with crayons

Phrase Making and Sentence Building from 2 to 3 Years

By the time kids reach 24 months, their vocabularies have doubled in size, and they begin pairing words to create two-word phrases and sentences, such as *want ball*. They haven't mastered all of the prepositions and "glue" words, but they are communicating with clarity and directness. Next, they start naming the subjects of their sentences, maybe adding an article (*a, an, the*) here and there, and using some verb endings, like *-s, -ed,* or *-ing*. They can point to the pictures and objects you say or that they see in a book. They can name people close to them and some body parts.

By 3 years old, kids may say up to three hundred words and understand even more. Their sentences may extend to four words or so, as phrases like *dog go* blossom into *the dog is going*. Counting aloud while pointing out objects is now a possibility, as is maneuvering puzzle pieces into place and climbing to reach things. Play gets more social. Little ones start watching and copying what their playmates are doing and may even (gasp!) share their toys a bit.

More verbs (*run, walk, fall, jump*) and more names for places and things (*house, park, cake*) emerge now, although longer words with more syllables and consonant clusters may still get clipped. An avocado may just be a *cado*, a banana a *nana*, a spider may be a *pider*, a squirrel a *skirl*. One helpful habit to shore up now is affirming and acknowledging whatever communication attempt they make. *Yes, that is the cup! Yes, it's a cat! Yes, grass!* Whatever they say can be followed with *yes*, plus a word and correct pronunciation of your own.

At this point, your little one's conceptual understanding may be taking off. They comprehend time and position (*today, tomorrow, in, on,* and *under*) and are full of questions, especially *why*. You have an opportunity here to step up your teaching in two big ways: explaining what words mean *and* nudging your toddler to use the words, too. You can facilitate this learning just by labeling the foods you eat, the clothes you put on, and the objects in your environment, as well as adding in some descriptive terms to scaffold their word knowledge. The *cold* water, the *rough* sandpaper, the *soft* pillow.

In choosing and sharing books, keep in mind that while there's a time and place for longer children's literature, you shouldn't overlook the power of five-minute stories read on a regular basis. It's not the length of the story but the cumulative impact of engaging with you and with print and oral language that enriches a child's life and skills. Many parents learn to love short, colorful books because they can read them in a minute. Knowing that you can make an impact in a minimal amount of time gives many parents the nudge they need to read to their child in the moment, versus putting it off in the hope of finding the "perfect" time.

Once you get started, you can always do repeated reading of the same books (toddlers love and benefit from repetition) or read multiple short stories. The key is just to get started.

SELECTED 2-TO-3-YEAR MILESTONES
Oral Language
- Says two-word here-and-now phrases and sentences, like *help shoe* and *dog bark*

- Produces lots of consonant sounds
- Knows the names of familiar people, items, and animals
- Follows basic directions, like *clean up* and *push your chair in*
- Asks simple questions, like *What's that?*
- Sings songs
- Claps syllables
- Hears and produces rhymes and alliteration
- Speaks /p/, /d/, /m/, /n/, /w/, and /h/ clearly
- Uses pronouns, like *my, me, mine, you, your, she, he,* and *we*
- Uses some prepositions, like *on* and *in*
- Speaks from 100 to 300 words
- Marks plurals with an *-s*
- Initiates turn-taking by saying *me* and *my turn*
- Talks to other kids

Book Behavior, Print Awareness, and Writing
- Enjoys looking at books independently
- Pretends to read familiar books
- Recalls book characters and straightforward storylines
- Recognizes logos in the environment (e.g., McDonald's)
- Identifies a letter or letters in their own name
- Points to and discusses pictures in books
- Scribbles with intentional circles and dots

Writing and Noticing Print from 3 to 4 Years

By age 3, kids typically know the names of family members, friends, and most objects in their daily lives. They understand prepositions (*on, in, under*), use some pronouns (*I, me, we*), and can string two or three sentences together. They know many words and their opposites.

Total strangers can even follow what they're saying. They're now full-on conversational partners who answer questions, respond to requests, and speak up if they feel cut off (*It's my turn!*).

At this point, they take up one of the most popular topics of everyday conversation: the weather. They notice and talk about the climate and precipitation, albeit without using those terms. You can see learning in action as they repeat tasks again and again to improve results. Whole jigsaw puzzles are now coming together, and they push and pull toy vehicles to get them moving. They can put like things with like—colors, shapes, toys, and objects—and count real-life objects like books on a table.

Their attention to and interest in longer stories takes off, and they can show off their comprehension by answering questions about what they just heard. They're speaking in longer sentences and linking those sentences' ideas together. They can follow (and appreciate) a clear storyline from beginning to middle to end. You can now ask questions during read-alouds that prompt them to think more, make predictions about what will come next, and connect stories to their own experiences.

You'll want to stick more closely to the text as printed on the page now, too, if you were prone to freestyling or skipping passages to keep their interest. Making print-to-speech connections is on their horizon now, so the verbal-written match should be more consistent. Also, be sure to read nonfiction titles, too, which grab kids' attention, pique their curiosity, and build their vocabularies.

If books and reading aloud have been a part of your family life since their infancy, your child may already recognize some letters, such as their own first initial. Begin gradually yet intentionally calling attention to more letters at this age—in isolation, in your daily environment, and in the books you read. Jot a solo letter on a piece of paper or call your child's attention to a monogrammed towel or an alphabet block for a mini-lesson.

Talk about the lines, curves, hooks, humps, and dots that form letters. This helps kids understand that a limited number of critical features form all letters. Point out the orientation of those features (horizontal, vertical, diagonal), and their size (height, width), too. This makes it easier for kids to recognize different letters and write them.

You can also start helping your child understand that certain printed shapes—letters—have names and indicate sounds by saying things like *S says /s/. S-A-M says Sam.* They won't get it at first, but repeating simple short sentences like this now and then over the days, weeks, and months of early childhood will deliver the message.

SELECTED 3-TO-4-YEAR MILESTONES
Oral Language and Sound Awareness
- Uses 1,000 words
- Asks for clarification
- Uses more pronouns: *they, us, hers, his, them, her, my, me, mine, you*
- Uses possessives: *dog's toy*
- Talks about objects and their functions
- Notices syllables in words
- Makes some letter-sound associations
- Makes and identifies rhymes
- Can isolate and compare initial letter sounds in words

Book Behavior, Print Awareness, Writing, and Letter Recognition
- Follows the structure of a story
- Makes predictions about what will happen next in a tale

- Connects text to personal experience
- Points to print as the source of information in a story
- Recognizes and prefers favorite book characters
- Understands that pictures are connected in a story
- Recognizes their own name in print, plus some familiar words
- Names letters on everyday objects, signs, and posters
- Makes letter-like scribbles to represent words
- Attempts to print their own name

Prereading from 4 to 5 Years

Little ones at this point can introduce themselves with first name and last, sing a song or nursery rhyme by heart, and tell a story of their own. Four-year-olds are well aware of cause and effect and have developed a good bit of sophistication around language and books. They begin comparing and contrasting favorite characters in different books. They come to see books as sources for answers to questions about the world.

It's time to build some print awareness by talking to your child about how books work, how print conveys meaning, and what words are. These are vital lessons, because before a child can read print, they must notice it. Sprinkle in a few comments (max) before or during reading that direct your child's attention to how books are organized and how print mirrors spoken language. Use your finger to point to letters and words, which helps them connect the print on the page with the speech they hear and understand.

SAMPLE PHRASES
- *These are the words. I need to read them from this side to this side.* (Trace finger from left to right along the text.)

- *Where should we start reading? Here?* (Point to the first word on the page.) *Or here?* (Point to the last word on the page.)
- *I know this is the top of the page. Show me where the bottom of the page is.*

Before you dive into a book, get in the habit of taking a few moments to consider the cover together, highlighting the title and author or illustrator names. Just point to the appropriate cover elements while describing what the words say and how they relate to the book.

It's obvious to us, as adults who are skilled readers, but the notion that books are read in a particular order, from front to back in English, is something kids must learn. Similarly, they must come to understand that we read English from the top of the page to the bottom and from left to right. They may recognize these print features eventually without you directly mentioning them, but there's evidence that pointing to words on the page increases the time 3-to-5-year-olds look at print (versus illustrations) in picture books. And attention to print is a precursor to the knowledge of page order, page organization, and print direction that we're after.

Then continue to direct their attention to print in books as they grow older, pointing out more and more features as time goes on. Books typically feature uppercase and lowercase versions of letters, as well as different fonts. State the letter names while pointing to each version, so your child can begin to connect the letter names to the uppercase and lowercase shapes, recognizing them as distinct representations of the same category. And books also illustrate the point that letters make up words, helping kids bridge into reading.

Recognizing words in print is another skill that's years in the making. Kids have to learn that letters are different from words, although some words have just one letter. They have to grasp that words have space between them in writing and that they carry meaning. And that's just what it takes to become aware of words as a general concept or category of print. Then they still have to do the hard work of recognizing particular words. Books give parents a convenient and fun way to gently call attention to these concepts again and again.

SELECTED 4-TO-5-YEAR MILESTONES

Oral Language and Phonemic Awareness

- Uses thousands of words and carries on conversations
- Asks *wh-* questions: *why, where, what, when, who*
- Responds to *wh-* questions
- Refers to quantities
- Uses conjunctions, like *when, so, if, because*
- Recognizes sounds that match and words that begin or end with the same sounds
- Recognizes and produces rhyming words
- Distinguishes, blends, and segments separate syllables in spoken words
- Recognizes single sounds and combinations of sounds

Book Behavior, Print Awareness, Writing, and Letter Recognition

- Writes their own name
- Identifies their own name in print
- Names some upper- and lowercase letters
- Understands cause and effect
- Follows story sequences
- Represents themself in drawings
- Forms letters

- Detects, manipulates, and analyzes speech sounds
- Recognizes the difference between letters and other symbols
- Recognizes some letters and their sounds in words, including their own name
- Uses writing to represent thoughts and spells phonetically

Emergent and Beginning Reading from 5 to 7 Years

At 5 and 6 years old, kids typically speak clearly, tell stories with complete sentences, use the future tense, and say their own full name and address. They can count past 10, draw a person with several body parts, and copy triangles and other shapes, and they know a good deal about everyday life, from food to money.

But real differences in their literacy skills become obvious (to them and us) at this point, too. Elementary school classrooms often put reading and writing on display in ways that can't help but highlight student variations. Everything from the reading group they're placed in to the work displayed on the bulletin board exposes the differences.

It can be agonizing for parents to hear about the social drama playing out in the name of education—tales of one child being put "on the computer" because they can't read, another checking out the same baby book from the classroom library every day because that's what's on "their level," and yet another signing their name with a scribble that's different every time.

Yet all of these kids are on their own unique paths to reading. We just need to clearly identify what they're working with, so that we may deliver the right experiences, instructions, and additional tools. A few quick definitions, based on what science reveals about how beginners learn to read words in and out of context, will help.

- **Prereaders** rely mainly on visuals and context clues to make sense of words. They may recognize a word within the context of a logo, say *Nike* or *McDonald's*, but they are unable to read those same words in regular type without the contextual clues of color or location. They do not yet use letter-sound cues to read or write.
- **Beginning or emergent readers**, sometimes called partial alphabetic readers, are *beginning* to apply what they know about letters and sounds to read and write. They know how most letters map to sounds, but can't yet decode unfamiliar words. They spell phonetically (*duz* for *does*, for example).
- **Alphabetic readers** have full command of letter-sound correspondences, can decode unfamiliar words, and can spell from memory.
- **Fluent readers, or consolidated alphabetic readers,** have forged a solid knowledge of many words' spellings, pronunciations, and meanings through deep experience of hearing, saying, spelling, and understanding them. They can read and spell words that have multiple syllables from memory.

SELECTED 5-TO-7-YEAR MILESTONES

Oral Language

- Retells stories in sequential order
- Talks about events
- Uses a range of adverbs and adjectives
- Asks and answers complex questions
- Gives directions

Book Behavior, Print Awareness, and Writing

- Writes full name

- Recognizes upper- and lowercase letters
- Connects letters to their sounds
- Tracks print from left to right
- Sounds out words
- Spells phonetically
- Reads and writes simple sentences
- Begins sentences with capital letters
- Attempts punctuation
- Correctly spells frequently used words

Fluent Reading and Deep Comprehension at Any Age

The ultimate level of reading we're aiming for is a moving target. The sophistication your child will need to thrive will depend on the individual goals they pursue in higher education, the demands of the workplaces they enter, and the invention of new technologies and media that we can't even imagine today.

The term *literacy* itself changes over time. From the dawn of tablets (stone, that is) millennia ago to the global proliferation of the electronic variety today, social and technological change has altered the very definition of the word. As parents, we need to be aware of literacy's dynamism as modes of communication change. I think of how my daughter's second-grade year was dramatically altered by COVID-19 stay-at-home orders and an influx of digital technology. A kid who'd had limited screen time suddenly spent *hours* online daily and became adept at classroom tech, videoconferencing, and ebook procurement—because she had to. The terms of engagement with her school, teacher, and classmates had been transformed in an instant. A pandemic raised educational stakes by activating new approaches to technology, communication, and learning.

The need to leverage skilled reading to meet contemporary needs endures. And the best readers, whether 8 or 80 years old, will be defined by their ability to identify the vast majority of words in any text they encounter and construct meaning from them, individually and collectively.

As each developmental stage illustrates, this level of comprehension is built on the foundation of a stimulated brain, a robust vocabulary, and wide-ranging written language experiences. To read well may take a lifetime, but it all starts from day one.

JOURNAL PROMPTS

- What new or funny things is your little one trying or doing?

- What are you focused on nurturing or teaching now?

- Where might you focus next?

- What people or resources can support you in raising your reader?

3

Yes You Can: Five Touchstones for Parents Who Dare to Teach

Those who can, do. Those who understand, teach.

—Lee S. Shulman

Reading is taught, not caught. This phrase has been in circulation for decades, but it bears repeating with each new generation of parents, and it has never been more fully supported by compelling evidence. Learning to read is a complex, unnatural, years-long odyssey, and parents should bear no illusions that their kids will pick it up merely by watching other people read or being surrounded by books.

In Chapters 1 and 2, you got a glimpse of how fascinating the twists and turns that lead to literacy are, how influential parents are in helping kids navigate them, and how early in life that power is in evidence. Now I offer five teaching tenets to carry with you. Don't worry, there are no scripted sequences, rigid rules, or worksheets forthcoming. These are principles any parent can remember and apply with ease during long, busy days with young children. Some of the five you may know instinctually. Others may have never crossed your mind. All deserve to be hallmarks of the way we approach raising readers.

These touchstones are research-backed and parent-approved. Personally, I've found that returning to these principles, even now that my daughter is a strong, fluent, and independent reader, still makes a difference for her, me, and our relationship. Ultimately, they are calls to be a more patient, more responsive, and more purposeful parent in every context.

May you find the same comfort, wisdom, and practical guidance in them that I did. Take them to heart. Repeat them like mantras if you like. And remember, the sooner you embrace them, the better this journey gets.

It's What You Say—*and* How You Say It

Spurring literacy development, like teaching of any kind, is about creating shared meaning between you and your little one. And that requires meeting them where they are, capturing their attention, engaging in back-and-forth exchanges, and also providing the stimulation that helps them to their next level.

Parents' actions such as asking questions vs. giving directives, introducing novel vocabulary, and arranging words and phrases in advanced ways all affect kids' language development. But parent responsiveness plays a major role as well, for example how reliably and enthusiastically you respond to your child's speech and actions. As Harvard pediatrics professor Jack Shonkoff puts it, "Reciprocal and dynamic interactions . . . provide what nothing else in the world can offer—experiences that are individualized to the child's unique personality style, that build on his or her own interests, capabilities, and initiative, that shape the child's self-awareness, and that stimulate the child's growth and development."

So we must have the awareness to let a child's age or language ability affect the content *and* tenor of our speech. Studies provide evidence that infants and young toddlers, for example, benefit from conversations about the here and now with us pointing and gesturing to label objects in our immediate surroundings or on the pages of books we're reading together. And *parentese* is the speaking style of choice. Slower, higher pitched, and more exaggerated than typical speech, it's been thought to advance infants' language learning because of the ways it simplifies the structure of language and evokes a response from babies.

With older toddlers and preschoolers, we should keep examining what we're saying and how, but update the range of things we consider. It's no longer necessary to speak at a slow pace or nearly an octave higher than normal to aid a child's language development. By 30 months, the variety and sophistication of parents' word choices may have a greater influence on kids' vocabulary growth. By 42 months, talking about things beyond the present, such as delving into memories of the past or discussions of what will happen in the future, is positively related to kids' vocabulary skills a year later.

While it's unnatural and unrealistic to monitor yourself all day, the thing to remember is that our words and responsiveness fuel powerful learning for kids. Set aside ten minutes a day of mindful communication, focusing on your baby, your words, and the interplay between them. Over time the focused practice will create habits that spill over into other conversations, too.

Learning Takes Time—and Space

We live in a catch-up culture, where people feel perpetually behind and forced to hustle near the finish line after being waylaid by hurdle after hurdle. This contributes to the (false) belief that we can make up in intensity what we lack in good pacing. But we can't cram kids' way to reading.

Ask any learning scientist about the relative merits of massing study together versus spreading it out over time. They'll tell you that spacing between sessions boosts retention of the material. The proof of the principle (known as *spaced learning, interleaving,* or *distributed practice*) shows up all over the place. Numerous studies across the human life span, from early childhood through the senior years, have documented its power. And there's evidence of the benefits of spaced study across a wide range of to-be-learned material, such as pictures, faces, and foreign language vocabulary and grammar. Even learners taking CPR courses performed better if their classes were spaced out. So if you want your child to remember what you're teaching, digging into it for ten minutes a day for three days likely will beat a half-hour deep dive. The spacing effect is among the field of psychology's most replicated findings.

Incidentally, a study found that a bias for massed learning emerges in kids in the early elementary school years, so you're in good company if the approach feels counterintuitive. In the preschool years, the kids were as likely to think learning something bit by bit over time was as effective as learning it in a clump. During elementary school, though, the kids started predicting that massed learning would be better at promoting memory than spaced learning.

Maybe the teaching methods employed in so many classrooms give kids (and parents) the impression that repetition, repetition, repetition in one sitting is the way knowledge sticks in memory. Want to learn your spelling words? *Write them over and over again in different colored pencils.* Want to practice your handwriting? *Fill that page with well-formed letters.*

Spacing things out may feel inefficient, but it's more effective, more fun, and a better fit for daily life with young kids. Parents have a natural advantage in teaching more gradually, because we are with kids for hours a day over the course of years. We aren't under intense time pressure, at least over the long term, removed as we are from the confines of a school day or school year. Nor do we have to find a way to meet the needs of twenty-five kids or more at once.

And keep in mind that the lessons we give needn't be formal. Teaching young children often looks like talking, playing, and singing. I once ordered a home spelling program that included what felt like 50 million individual magnetic letter tiles, color-coded index cards, and scripted teaching procedures. I was so tired from separating and organizing all the materials that I never got around to working through the curriculum with my daughter.

Ultimately, conversation over a few games of prefix bingo one week taught her more about prefixes, suffixes, and units of meaning within words than the elaborate curriculum did. Why? Because that was the method I enjoyed and followed through on—the one that worked within the context of our relationship and our attention spans. She loves board games; I love talking about words. Win-win.

The takeaway: do what works for you, and do it a little at a time.

The More Personal the Lesson, the Better

Helping your child learn to read requires making decision after decision. Which letters or words to teach? Which song to sing or story to tell? When making the calls, err on the side of making the lessons themselves personally meaningful for your child. Sometimes it's as straightforward as teaching the child the letters in their name first, making up songs and stories featuring their pets, or choosing vocabulary words from their favorite books. Sometimes it's as deep as practicing fluency by reading aloud texts that affirm and sustain a child's cultural heritage or community.

To help conceptualize this, researchers have defined three levels of personal relevance, from mere *association* to *usefulness* to *identification*. When a reading lesson centers on a passage about the student's sport of choice (say, soccer), that's making a personal association. If you can make it clear how the lesson itself is useful for advancing a goal the child is after (like joining wordplay with older siblings), even better. But if you can make the activity resonate with the child's sense of self, you're really cooking with grease. This is what's going on when a little one named Anna sees the letter A and says, *That's my letter!* She's owning it—and identifying with it. It matters to her and she learns it quickly.

The power of personal meaning also helps explain why parents so often find that something that worked like a charm with one child falls flat with another. Kids' associations, judgments of usefulness, and identities vary widely, even when they grow up under the same roof. Locking in on what makes your individual learner tick and facilitating resonant experiences just for them is golden.

Luckily, you have a built-in feedback mechanism for determining what's working: your child. Even infants express preferences. A little one might reach for the same book with bold illustrations or lift-up flaps over and over again. You may also find that what gives the lesson meaning is *you*—your demeanor, your engagement, and your responsiveness can be tremendous motivators.

Praise the Process

You're voluntarily reading a parenting book, so I'll venture that you value learning and have confidence that you'll reap some benefit from the effort you put into acting on the tips compiled here. You believe that you can know more, teach better, and make an impact. And I imagine that you want your child to feel the same sense of self-assurance as they pursue their own challenges.

One way to cultivate that can-do spirit is by cheering on their hard work, focus, and determination by name. Instead of giving generic praise like "You're so smart," say specifically what you loved about *how* they learned—not just the results. For example, if your little one is beginning to write letters: "Great job picking up the pencil and writing. I see you working to hold it in your grasp." You'll celebrate their work and lay the motivational track for other efforts to come.

Research by psychologist Carol Dweck and others has found evidence that when parents praise kids' effort in the learning process—not outcomes—it impacts their kids' belief that they can improve their ability with effort. With that growth mindset, they are more likely to think they can get smarter if they work at it, a trait that boosts learning and achievement.

In a longitudinal study, Dweck and colleagues traced the whole path of these relations, from parents uttering things like "Good job working hard" when their kids were 1 to 3 years old, to testing those same kids' academic achievement in late elementary school. They found evidence that this process-related praise predicted a growth mindset in children, which contributed to strong performance in math and reading comprehension later on in fourth grade. The study also found evidence that parents established their praise style (more process-focused, or less so) early on. So learn how to give meaningful compliments. The positive vibes leave lasting impressions.

When in Doubt, Look It Up

This was my dad's go-to saying when I peppered him with questions as a kid. A good reference guide, in our case a giant *Webster's* dictionary that he kept on a wooden stand in his office, was always the first stop for a spelling, definition, or example. His words remain with me, reminding me how important it is to continue learning as we endeavor to teach our kids. My dad didn't have all the answers and wasn't afraid to learn alongside me.

When it comes to nurturing and teaching reading, we should stay curious and work to deepen our content knowledge, versus falling back on instructional methods that are more familiar than effective. For example, parents often do things like tell kids to sound out words like *right*, *people*, and *sign* that can't be, well, sounded out. These words clearly don't feature direct letter-sound matches, but our default response to any decoding question, phonetic or not, is "sound it out." The lesson a child needs in those instances isn't how to blend this letter sound into that one, but how the English language and its writing system work overall.

Similarly, if we decide to teach spelling, we should make it a priority to learn something about word origins and get a handle on conventional letter-sequence patterns. Having a child write a word over and over again is *one method*, but it's one you'll probably feel more comfortable letting go of as you know more about *why* we spell how we do. Fear not, pointers on how to talk about words and spelling in ways that both boost your confidence and deepen kids' understanding are coming up in Chapter 9.

When we're well informed about how written English works and how reading develops, we can take advantage of the countless teachable moments in everyday life. So, without further ado, the following chapters will help you learn what you need to teach with confidence.

—————————JOURNAL PROMPTS—————————

- What cues can you employ to speak well, praise process, and make lessons personal? Make a list of actions you'll try, such as turning your phone ringer off at dinnertime to reduce distraction or taking a breath before answering when your child asks a question to make sure you respond thoughtfully and helpfully. Then circle the item on your list that you'll try first.

- How can you set up your physical environment to remind you to nurture literacy bit by bit, day by day? Brainstorm your own list of things to try, such as putting magnetic letters on the fridge, hanging a nursery rhyme mobile over the changing table, or posting an alphabet chart on the wall.

- What's likely to stand in the way of you doing these things consistently? Can you imagine, plan for, and overcome the obstacles?

4

You're Hired: Essential Lessons Every Parent Can—and Should—Give Kids

Whatever the intellectual quality of the education given our children, it is vital that it include elements of love and compassion, for nothing guarantees that knowledge alone will be truly useful to human beings.

—His Holiness the Fourteenth Dalai Lama

Humans have been reading at least since the late fourth millennium BCE, when pictographic script was first etched into clay tablets with the original stylus, a writing tool sharp enough to leave an impression. And explicit reading instruction in English—directly teaching the links between letters and sounds—has been going on since the sixteenth century. But it's just been in the last several decades that we've had the benefit of rigorous experiments, massive data sets, and targeted technologies to illuminate the earliest *roots* of reading and parents' critical role in sustaining them. Perhaps this new knowledge can push us from literacy for the elite to literacy for all.

In this chapter, we'll explore six prereading and early reading subject areas that parents are especially well equipped to teach kids with love and lightness in daily life. They include oral language, speech-sound awareness, and letter knowledge skills that research shows are critically important for later reading skills. Plus, we'll cover the simple work of familiarizing kids with books and how print works, as well as the more advanced work of matching letters to sounds (and sounds to letters).

Although abilities like these tend to show up in preschool and kindergarten screenings, they apply to a much wider age span—I'd say from birth to 116, given the remarkable story of a woman named Mary Walker, born in 1848.

Walker's dream of literacy, beautifully told in Rita Lorraine Hubbard's picture book *The Oldest Student: How Mary Walker Learned to Read*, was deferred through slavery and sharecropping, through the lives of two husbands and three sons, and the administrations of twenty-six presidents of the United States. She learned at last at 116 years old, and read until her death at age 121 on December 1, 1969.

"She studied the alphabet until her eyes watered," Hubbard wrote. "She memorized the sounds each letter made and practiced writing her name so many times that her fingers cramped . . . She studied and studied, until books and pages and letters and words swirled in her head while she slept. One fine day Mary's hard work paid off. She could read!"

Literacy is still deferred for too long for too many, for lack of a strong foundation. I know a high school literacy coach whose job is to give teachers strategies to help teenagers *who can't read* to make sense of the science, math, social studies, and other lessons they receive at school. Imagine being expected to learn advanced content with no understanding of the printed information in textbooks and classroom materials. When she can, she pulls students out of class to tutor them in the basics of letter-sound associations that they never mastered in elementary or middle school. It's not a service she expected to provide high schoolers but one they desperately need. And who will be there to help them when they struggle after they graduate—or drop out?

Would-be readers of any age must master the basics. There are areas of study that just cannot be skipped. Here are six knowledge areas that learners of any age can visit, revisit, and master to become more successful readers, plus ways parents can build and reinforce each.

Oral Language

Spoken words are the precursor of all precursors to reading. When learning to read, a child can't make sense of a word in print that they haven't heard before in life. So parents must carry on conversations from the beginning to build up kids' word banks. Research provides evidence that the better children's vocabularies at kindergarten entry, the better their reading comprehension in third grade, and the better their third-grade reading skills, the better their high school graduation rates. Whatever your child's age, they'll benefit from more conversation with you.

For optimal brain development, aim for 40 "conversational turns" per hour when you're with your little one. It counts as a turn whenever you greet one of your baby's coos, babbles, words, or sentences with a verbal response (or they verbally respond to your words) within 5 seconds. It's tough to get an exact count, of course, without feedback from a "talk pedometer" like those used by researchers. Just know that most parents speak a lot less than they should—and a lot less than they think they do. The lesson here is: give your child the best shot at better vocabulary by taking every conversational turn you can. Chapters 5 and 6 delve more deeply into this topic.

Sound Awareness

If knowing the power of back-and-forth talk is parent priority number one, then understanding that kids need to learn to discern speech sounds within words is a close second. As experienced, fluent readers, we've taught ourselves to distinguish individual words and sounds that in fact don't exist as distinctly when spoken. If someone says, *I hear a symphony*, we think we hear four words, six syllables, and twelve or more sounds. But that's an understanding we've layered over a continuous stream of speech that a newborn might hear as simply *Ihearasymphony*. The sounds within words and the words themselves often run together with no clear boundaries between one and the next.

A child can understand a sentence without labeling it a sentence. They can grasp the declaration's meaning without having conscious awareness that it's made of individual words. And whether or not kids are aware of the presence of individual words, they focus on the message of the sentence as a whole, not the blending, blurring, and clustering of vowel and consonant sounds *within* the words. That's a different skill altogether.

Called *phonological awareness*, this "ability to recognize, discriminate, and manipulate the sounds in one's language" is crucial for learning to read. It spans from the recognition of syllables in words down to finer-grained discernment of individual speech sounds (called phonemes) like the initial /b/ sound in *banana*. Think of it as a single ability that plays out in a range of skills at different levels—the skill of clapping out the three syllables in *banana* would represent a beginning level, and the skill of replacing the initial /b/ sound with /f/ to turn *banana* into *fanana* as a part of a song or game would represent a more advanced level.

Parents can teach phonological awareness with prompts like the following:

Identifying: "Clap for each syllable in *cupcake*."
Blending: "What word is this: *cup . . . cake*?"
Segmenting: "What sounds do you hear in *cupcake*?"
Deleting: "Say *cupcake* without the *cup*."

It takes years to acquire this full range of phonological awareness, as children grow and develop in their ability to hear, speak, and understand language. And it's crucial for parents to attend to the skill early because research provides evidence that kids' ability to parse words at the individual speech-sound level (known as phonemic awareness) is closely related to early growth in word reading skills.

A 5-year-old who can't clap out the syllables in a word, blend together a few sounds, or tell you that *apple* starts with an /a/ sound will have trouble in school. Yet few parents know what specific sound-recognition skills they should be building when kids are 2, 3, and 4 years old—or how. (See Chapter 7 to find out.) As a mom who'd spent a fortune on reading tutoring for her young son lamented to me, too often parents hear about learning targets only after their children have missed them.

Print Awareness

Books are a handy tool for teaching an abstract concept—that the lines and curves kids see printed on paper, on products, and on signs mean something. Reading together with children presents a great opportunity to bring their attention to letters, words, and the conventions around how they are used. With just our voices and pointer fingers, we can teach the names and roles of key book features (such as *author* and *title*) and the direction we read English text (left to right, top to bottom). And it's important that we do so with preschool-aged children because researchers have found evidence for a causal relationship between their increased contact with print (from teachers, verbal and nonverbal references to text during shared reading four times weekly, for thirty weeks) and their reading, spelling, and comprehension skills two years later.

Teaching about print really is as easy as saying phrases like the following as you lift the cover, turn the pages, and point to relevant print features (no planning or preparation required):

- *Look at the words here on the book's cover.* (Point to the words.)
- *This is the title of the book.* (Point to the book's title.) *It says* Little Leaders: Bold Women in Black History. *What is the title of the book?*
- *The person who wrote the book is called the author. These words are the author's name.* (Point to the author's name.) *It says* Vashti Harrison.
- *This is where the bunny is talking. The bunny's words are inside this bubble.* (Point to speech bubble.)

In time, you can check your child's knowledge with questions and requests like: *Where do I start reading? Show me the author's name. Point to the last line.*

Also keep in mind that you don't have to have a book in hand to draw attention to print. There's a lot of competition for attention on a picture-book page—colors; illustrations; and even flaps, mirrors, and lift-up tabs. You might find better success teaching some elements of print in isolation. Show some love to the solo word or letter on a sheet of paper, a name on a sign, or a saying on a graphic tee. There are plenty of chances to bring letters to life by noticing, pointing out, and discussing their features and meaning with kids.

Letter Knowledge

As experienced readers, it's easy for us to forget that letters are just arbitrary marks on paper. The collections of dots, lines, and circles could mean anything. It's a process to learn to distinguish letters from pictures. It's also a challenge to remember which letter is which. After all, b and d, for example, *are* quite similar-looking.

In one of my absolute favorite picture books, *An Inconvenient Alphabet*, Beth Anderson explores the arbitrariness of our letters in genius fashion as she recounts the true story of Ben Franklin and Noah Webster's shared belief that English has letters with too many sounds (think: the /g/, /j/, and /f/ sounds in *goat, giraffe*, and *laugh*), sounds with too many letters (the /k/ sound in *chorus, kite, cat*, and *quiet*), and some letters that just aren't needed at all (the silent letters in *lamb, walk, knock*, and *give*).

Letters themselves, the twenty-six we know, plus others Franklin created that never took off, are important characters in the book. Designed to represent the sounds *aw, uh, edh, ing, ish*, and *eth*, Franklin's novel (and unpopular) letters are depicted as 3D models, carried around in a sack, and handed out for examination. When I read the book with my daughter, she anticipated objections to the new letters—they look funny, would be tough to learn, and would make old books harder to read.

I share this story to underscore the fact that letters—their names, shapes, and sounds—are wonderful subjects of study, far beyond repeated renditions of "The Alphabet Song." Pointing them out, describing their features, providing opportunities for kids to scribble or write them, and asking kids to name them or utter their sounds are all instructive. (There's also evidence that teaching kids to identify letters at 2 or 3 years old predicts letter knowledge in kindergarten.) And you can set the tone of curiosity and enthusiasm that makes letter exploration fun, not rote. Chapter 8 shows you how.

Letter-to-Sound Connections (aka Phonics)

Kids need to know about letters and discern the speech sounds within words. But that's not all: they also need to be able to reliably recall which letters make which sounds so they can decode the print they see.

That's why the best *initial* reading instruction in English directly teaches kids the links between letters and sounds, also known as phonics. It's a basic fact of English that the sounds of the language are represented by the letters of the alphabet. Grasping the connection between the symbols and sounds is a necessary step that puts children well on their way to reading. Memorizing whole words one by one, not so much.

Don't let the fact that some words can't be sounded out phonetically (*chef*, *yacht*, and *people*, for a few) dissuade you from teaching phonics. High-quality comprehensive reviews across the English-speaking world, from the United States to the UK to Australia, agree:

directly teaching the relationships between letters or letter combinations and the sounds they represent helps kids learn to read.

You can start by pointing out individual letters in books or your environment and sharing the sounds each makes, e.g., *The letter A says /a/. Like in* apple. Focus on the most common sound for the letter, for example, /k/ for c as in *canvas* (not /s/ as in *census*).

Jessica Toste, an associate professor in the College of Education at the University of Texas at Austin, told me that letter sounds are so helpful to know prior to kindergarten that she gives a cheat sheet to friends with young children. Titled "What Sound?," it lists the highest frequency letter-sound correspondences because many parents haven't isolated letter sounds in a very long time, she explains, or were never taught letter sounds themselves.

The teaching routine for parents is straightforward: Point to a letter and ask, *What sound?* If the child gets it right, say, *Great work matching the letter to its sound.* If they get it wrong, give them a correction, *The letter V says /v/.* Then ask them again, *What sound?* You can make the activity playful by passing a fake microphone back and forth or asking the question in a silly voice—whatever engages your child.

Pro tip: clip consonant sounds so that you don't confuse the issue with vowel sounds. For example, try to pronounce the letter K as a short /k/ sound versus "kuh."

Down the road, you can start helping your child blend the letters together, which is what we mean when we tell early readers to "sound out" words. You might say: *The sounds /d/, /o/, and /g/ make* dog. Or you can start with whole words and teach kids to break the words down into their sound and letter parts. *What sounds do you hear in* dog? Either way can work; understanding the relationship between letters and sounds is "necessary and nonnegotiable" in the

WHAT SOUND?

a	/a/	apple
b	/b/	book
c	/k/	cat
d	/d/	dog
e	/e/	egg
f	/f/	fish
g	/g/	goat
h	/h/	hat
i	/i/	igloo
j	/j/	jump
k	/k/	kite
l	/l/	love
m	/m/	mouse

n	/n/	nest
o	/o/	octopus
p	/p/	pig
q	/kw/	queen
r	/r/	rabbit
s	/s/	sun
t	/t/	tiger
u	/u/	up
v	/v/	van
w	/w/	win
x	/ks/	fo<u>x</u>
y	/y/	yarn
z	/z/	zebra

Practicing letter <u>sounds</u> as often as possible supports mastery and fluency. Focus on the highest frequency sound that each letter makes (e.g., /k/ for c, rather than /s/). Use cue words to help.

INSTRUCTIONAL ROUTINE

Place card with letter "c" on table in front of child.
Teacher: **What sound?**
Student: /k/
(Repeat with other letter sounds, out of alphabetical order. Provide multiple repetitions for short vowel sounds as students tend to need the most practice with these.)

IMMEDIATE FEEDBACK

If correct:
Right, /b/. Nice job!
What's a word that starts with /b/?

If incorrect or "I don't know":
The letter "b" makes the sound /b/. What sound? (Child repeats)
Right, /b/. Well done!

process of learning to read in every alphabetic writing system. As your child begins to understand these connections, they'll gain curiosity and confidence to push further into reading.

Your child won't have to laboriously translate letters into sounds one by one forever, just as you don't. But they do need to have this skill down pat before they can move to more fluently and rapidly recognizing words in print. Even after they're advanced, or expert, readers like you, they will continue to need the sound-to-letter blueprint to decode unfamiliar words. Always and forever. Letter-sound knowledge gives kids an indispensable tool for accessing print. From there, they gain more and more experience and learn to make sense of the symbols, sounds, and (crucially) their meaning. Chapter 8 dives into letter names, shapes, and sounds.

Sound-to-Letter Connections (aka Spelling)

Many parents don't think about teaching spelling until lists of "irregular" and high-frequency words get sent home in their elementary schoolers' backpacks to "practice" (aka memorize) at home. But ideally, it should be on your radar long before your child is ready for spelling quizzes, or even real reading.

From the beginning, encourage young children to attempt spelling by having paper and pencils handy, as well as by incorporating writing into imaginary play or games. Their creative "spellings" will progress from scribbles to letter-like scrawls to recognizable letters and ultimately readable words. Along the way, they'll gain valuable experience and motor skills, while also giving you insight into their understanding of phonemes, letters, and the connections between the two. Demonstrating writing in daily life, such as when you jot down a shopping list or pen a letter to a friend and explain the reason for the writing, is also a useful lesson.

For teaching "sight words" (in this case, high-frequency words with spelling-to-sound irregularity), it's likely that "detailed study of the letters in the word and their sequence—with a focus on the difficult parts—and linking this with the word's pronunciation" is a winning alternative approach to rote memorization. And the good news is parents can start exploring and explaining words and their spellings long before word lists and spelling spirals make their way home. Chapter 9 covers this in depth.

Are there other things that parents can and should do to nurture literacy? Absolutely. But these are six meaningful, life-altering, often-overlooked areas that are well within our capacity to start addressing (and, yes, *teaching*) today.

JOURNAL PROMPTS

- Which of the six interrelated instructional areas (oral language, sound awareness, print awareness, letter knowledge, phonics, and spelling) do you feel most confident to teach? Why?

- Which instructional areas will you need the greatest support in teaching?

- How will your engagement in the nurturing of preliteracy and literacy skills make your child's life better?

- What are the risks of not proactively nurturing your child's skills?

5

Nourishing Words: The Lasting Impact of Early Language

Our children cannot dream unless they live, they cannot live unless they are nourished, and who else will feed them the real food without which their dreams will be no different from ours?
—Audre Lorde

Some time ago, I read an unusual report from the Canterbury region of New Zealand. It told, in the subdued tone of an academic journal article, the story of an urgent rescue mission. On September 4, 2010, a massive earthquake rocked the city of Christchurch (population: 350,000). The seismic event measured 7.1 in magnitude. It tripped circuit breakers at substations and knocked out power. Building facades collapsed, crushed cars, and jammed roads. And that was just the warmup. For the next year and a half, the devastation continued, with ten thousand aftershocks and three more full-blown earthquakes. A violent quake in February of the following year killed 185 people and leveled the central business district.

But the report that caught my attention wasn't about the first responders who rushed in to tend to the injured, restore power, provide water, and reopen transport. It wasn't about the elaborate emergency-management structures that launched within hours. It was about an unheralded cadre working to address another type of fallout from the earthquakes, one a lot less visible than liquefied soil sending buried pipes floating to the surface.

The rescuers I read about were psychologists, health advisors, and educators, all collaborating to pilot a program aimed at preventing a crisis they foresaw for children affected by the earthquakes. They knew that life in extreme instability, whether wrought by war or famine or natural disaster, breeds developmental difficulties and re-inforces inequities, with lasting consequences. They had seen data, collected 6,000 miles away in Santiago, Chile, that suggested that an earthquake can create educational aftershocks, too. Preschool kids who took early-language and early-literacy assessments shortly after the earthquake occurred performed worse on letter-word identification and text comprehension than comparable kids who took the same assessments one year before the earthquake occurred. The study provided evidence that their performance had been hurt by their parents' disaster-wrought stress and their own. Plus, school-entry data back in New Zealand revealed that many kids living in earthquake-affected communities struggled with expressive language and aware-ness of sound structure in words. The researchers who ran the pilot program summed up the nature of the challenge with characteristic understatement: "These results suggest that such experiences may impact families, with potential developmental sequelae for children."

But before vulnerable kids' development can rebound, parents, teachers, and other concerned parties must *notice* the learning crises, which aren't glaring like abandoned buildings with missing windows and walls. Next, we have to sustain interest and intentional action through a yearslong recovery, without the benefit of construction clamor to herald our progress.

The fact is, on any given day in any given community—natural disaster or not—there are learning crises brewing. There are children who aren't getting the language they need, due to household disorder and chaos, parent disposition, and a range of other circumstances. And although poverty creates the kind of stress and instability that lessen child-focused conversation and responsiveness in homes, many well-educated and advantaged families struggle with talk, too, for any number of reasons. Across demographics, differences in language skills are associated with differences in healthcare outcomes, high school graduation rates, job placement results, earning levels, and more.

The central truth every parent must grasp is this: oral-language skills are required for reading. Just as kids crawl before they walk, they talk before they read. And before they talk, babies listen, grunt, and coo. We must facilitate and encourage it all.

As language development expert Roberta Michnick Golinkoff and colleagues put it, "Language is causally implicated in most of what children learn in the first years of life. Indeed, kindergarten language scores, which are deeply rooted in the language development of infants and toddlers, are the single best predictor of school achievement in all subjects in third and fifth grade."

Psychologists Anne E. Cunningham and Jamie Zibulsky describe the delayed strong influence of early oral-language skills and reading development as a kind of "sleeper effect." The importance of early oral-language skills should not be underestimated, they say, because "no matter how accurately a middle school student can sound out new and difficult words like *omniscient* or *prejudice*, his ability to understand these words in context will depend on how often he has talked about these words and the concepts related to them. Each new word that a child acquires verbally becomes a word that he will eventually be able to recognize and make sense of when he sees it in print, so early vocabulary development is an essential skill for later reading success."

Think back to the overlapping, interrelated language and learning processes described in Chapter 2. They are like one of those elaborate domino creations that garner millions of views on YouTube. A creator devotes weeks to meticulously placing domino after domino into an elaborate design, just to engineer a few minutes of excitement when the first block sets off a chain reaction that topples thousands more. Some tumble in a straight line. Others, placed at a slight angle, bend the pattern into curves and turns. Still others are positioned to hit two dominos at once, sending branches of the design off in different directions.

Early parent talk is the first domino. It pings (through years of back-and-forth conversation) straight into an infant's grunts, coos, babbles, and eventually words. At the same time, those early conversations knock down other dominos and create a new branch at the split that builds momentum toward a toddler's vocabulary, which affects school readiness, which predicts third-grade reading, which correlates with high school graduation rates, and so on.

The influence that frequent, quality parent talk has on eventual literacy is so strong and begins so early in life that many experts now rank it above the once be-all, end-all practice of reading aloud. In fact, some argue that talking with your child from infancy may be "the single strongest action you can take to increase your child's educational opportunities." Language learning starts early—in utero, by about 35 weeks gestation—and the formation of synapses involved in language learning peaks during the first 6 months after birth. Researchers in one study found evidence that the richness of a child's early-language environment predicts their vocabulary, their language and speech processing, and fourth-grade literacy outcomes better than their mothers' education level or family welfare status.

Words matter. Timing matters. You matter.

Language Nutrition Defined

We talk to our kids for all kinds of reasons in the moment—to soothe, to encourage, to entertain, to direct. And there's power in every word we speak, including the impromptu conversations we have while giving baths, making meals, and playing at home. But sometimes we go above and beyond, delivering a kind of fortified talk that's extra nourishing to their long-term brain, language, and social development.

Some early-language advocates call this "language nutrition" to emphasize just how vital it is. You may even have had such a coaching session at the pediatrician's office, with a nurse or doctor modeling how to talk to a baby, inviting the parents to do the same, and then encouraging them to practice the techniques at home.

I experienced such a doctor's visit when my daughter was 3 years old, and I'll admit I found it puzzling at first. We'd just relocated to Texas and were due for a well-child appointment at a new pediatric practice. Without any preamble, the doctor locked gaze with my daughter, introduced herself, and then directed all the exam questions to Zora. I felt sidelined and devalued as a source of information about my daughter's health, but that was far from the doctor's intention. I had no way of knowing it, but in addition to giving a medical exam she was modeling rich language, another kind of prescription for a child's well-being. The doctor had just forgotten that as a new patient I needed a bit of orientation to the practice.

In Georgia, a statewide campaign called Talk With Me Baby

teaches obstetric, neonatal, and pediatric nursing students to coach parents and caregivers on language nutrition in a child's first years of life. They use the *I Do. We Do. You Do.* method. In the *I Do* step, nurses model how to talk with a baby by themselves directly addressing the baby, saying things like "Hi, baby! It's so good to see you. How are you feeling today?" In the *We Do* step of the protocol, the nurse invites the parent into the conversation with the baby and shares tips on why and how to talk to little ones. Finally, in the *You Do* step, the nurse passes the baton to the parent to keep up the child-directed talk and provides feedback and encouragement.

The takeaways? Your speech is an essential part of the environment your child inhabits and learns from. To make the most impact on a child's development, speak directly to them in infancy and early childhood. The quantity, variety, and responsiveness of the words you share with them influences the size of their vocabulary and the speed of its growth. Watch and listen for their communication, however subtle—a coo, a reach, a cry—and respond wholeheartedly, with words, expressions, and gestures of your own to keep the dialogue going.

Brains differ at birth, even among some twins from the same egg, who aren't 100 percent genetically identical at birth. Newborns vary widely in their processing of sights and sounds, as well as in their speed of responses to stimuli—but it's their environment that makes these differences trivial or meaningful in the long run, states Usha Goswami, director of the Centre for Neuroscience in Education at the University of Cambridge. "Usually, as long as the environment is rich enough, sufficient learning experiences enable less efficient brains to reach similar developmental end points to more efficient brains," Goswami states.

From infancy, children are active, engaged learners. They choose where to look, and they make bids for the attention of the people around them by wriggling and crying. A parent who responds by swaddling them in a blanket, handing them a toy, or empathizing with a gesture of their own nurtures the child as a person and a learner. The caregiver who makes a habit of reacting with immediacy, warmth, and words sets an incredible trajectory for cognitive, social, and emotional growth.

That's welcome news for everyone who wants to make a difference beyond the genetics you contributed to your child's makeup. Your talk and responses count significantly among the learning experiences they need. The process is verbal, but it's also interpersonal. You feed your child language within the context of your relationship. The love and meaning you share deepen the impact of your words.

Talk Like This

Beyond the quantity of words you speak, *the way* you speak them affects different aspects of your child's language and literacy development. Here are the chief characteristics of nourishing early caregiver language and how they help kids learn:

- *Child-Directed:* Your words are delivered expressly to and for the child, as opposed to language they pick up indirectly through overheard adult conversations or media. Child-directed speech supports language learning because it provides much more than words. It pairs content with helpful physical, social, and other cues.
- *Melodic:* Your delivery is clear, high-pitched, and with more exaggerated vowels than the way you might address adults.

Many moms do this naturally, even taking prosody to the point of parody. And for good reason—infants prefer listening to this "baby talk," and that attention may support their ability to discern the sounds within words as well as recognize word boundaries and grammatical units.

- *Loving:* Your words and gestures are warm, affectionate, and encouraging, versus stern commands or brusque movements. New research related to how emotion is expressed through movement suggests that by 11 months old kids can detect whether actions like grasping an item are performed with happy or angry motions—and shows that they match what they observe with happy or angry facial expressions of their own.

- *Home Language:* You speak in the language you know best, not necessarily the dominant language of your neighborhood or the school your child will attend. This is so that you can give your child the richest vocabulary, most fluent speech, and deepest background knowledge to support learning in any language.

- *Repetitive:* You use consistent names and labels for the people and things in your child's environment, so your little one gets many opportunities to distinguish among words in the stream of speech, make the connections between words, and discern word meanings. You also frame sentences with short, familiar phrases like *Look at the* ___, *That's a* ___, *Where is the* ___?, and *There's the* ___. The setup and repetition help toddlers grasp common nouns.

- *Expressive:* You point to the things you're referring to and match your facial expressions to your words. The body movements capture infant attention and give helpful context for the meaning of what you say, which boosts learning.

- *Responsive:* You listen well and provide feedback that's contingent on your little one's babbles, words, facial expressions, and gestures. This quality of interaction is predictive of kids' language achievements. You also give your little one plenty of time and space to receive what you communicate and to express themselves, too. There's evidence that by 11 months, infants coordinate their gaze, vocalizations, and gestures to intentionally communicate with caregivers. If your baby is staring at a fire truck or touching your sweater, you might say, *Oh, yes, a red fire truck.* Or *Feel the sweater. Isn't it soft?*

The nourishment that language provides when parents and children feed one another words, attention, and contingent responses is like a holiday feast spread over many courses, punctuated with lively rounds of conversation and laughter. Unlike the dense, compact nutrition of an energy bar, it's meant to be savored.

How Reading Aloud Fortifies Talk

None of this emphasis on early talk with kids should dampen your enthusiasm for reading aloud. In fact, reading picture books to and with kids boosts their oral-language experience by introducing more (and more diverse) vocabulary. Researchers at the Ohio State University in collaboration with the Columbus Metropolitan Library estimated that kids whose parents read them five board or picture books a day would have heard 1.4 million more words during storybook reading by age 5 than children who were never or seldom read to. Other studies have found that the vocabulary within picture books is more novel, challenging, and enriching than what's typically heard in everyday family conversation.

Moreover, a particular style of book sharing called "rich reading" by the New Zealand team that responded to the earthquake learning crisis can encourage high-quality conversation. It's a style of reading aloud that fosters comment and discussion as parents talk about the illustrations, label the characters' emotions, relate the content of the story to their child's life, and generally find ways to heighten the child's engagement with the tale, as well as their awareness of the text conveying it.

Reading with babies especially is a sensory, dynamic, visceral experience, and an efficient vehicle for the back-and-forth language we're going for. Every part of the exchange is novel for the infant—the smell of the book, the feel of the pages, and the motion as you move from cover to cover. Not to mention the look of the text and images on the page, and the words, sounds, and gestures they elicit from their parent.

With so much going on, where should a parent focus during storytime? On the relationship, I say. For the first year of your child's life, don't worry about teaching. Stay in nurture mode. Hold your baby close. Tune in to their responses. Lean in to their coos, babbles, kicks, and giggles, and return it all with as much vocabulary-rich talk as you can muster. You can't go wrong when you open a book, read, and follow the child's lead.

As your little one grows into a toddler, preschooler, and beyond, books can help them learn all kinds of things, from sound awareness and letter knowledge to story structure and science. The possibilities for meaningful, expansive conversation are endless when a well-chosen book, enthusiastic parent, and engaged child commune. Visit readingforourlives.com/books for a list of recommended reads for each age and stage.

Cultivate Mindfulness

Once we know the impact of oral language, the challenge is to live it. For me, it's helpful to think of parental speech and interaction as one dimension of the broader practice of mindfulness—consciously paying attention to the present moment. I first studied mindfulness meditation in a stress-reduction class hosted by the health center at my college. As an anxious overachiever, I was fascinated by the idea that you could experience the events of your life without being fully immersed in or carried away by them. I took a similar course a decade later, as a new mom recovering from major knee surgeries and trying to manage the pain—and my resulting irritability. I practiced finding a sliver of perspective in any given moment and conjuring the space to create more-helpful responses to whatever life brought my way.

I studied mindfulness meditation as a strategy for high-stress, high-pressure, high-stakes situations, but I now appreciate its value in every aspect of life (and parenting). The careful observation of our own thoughts, words, and deeds gives us the consciousness we need to discern what's helpful, powerful, or useful in any moment. With that awareness, we learn to wield our words in ways that heighten kids' understanding of language's meaning and function. And, even beyond the nuts and bolts of literacy building, we gain a greater capacity to speak in ways that nurture and sustain our children as whole people. As meditation teacher Joseph Goldstein puts it, "Part of mindfulness is calling to mind or remembering what is skillful, what is unskillful . . . and so we're really developing a wisdom about ourselves, our hearts, our minds, our lives."

This perspective has profound implications. When we can see what's constructive and what's not, we then have the option to consciously continue or discard our patterns. And even more—we have a chance to create new, more constructive ones, so that in the future we can do the good work automatically.

The Other Why

Another reason to focus on nurturing a strong oral-language environment from day one is that it's a proven stress reducer—for you. Tuning in to your baby, heightening awareness of their bids for attention, and engaging with them in back-and-forth conversations as they learn language actually reduces parenting stress, according to a study of moms who faced the typical stresses associated with childrearing *plus* household financial strain.

In this study, moms who received coaching around how to read with their kids and how to infuse more nourishing language into their routines reported levels of stress reduction typically associated with interventions explicitly designed for that purpose—things like therapy or direct instruction in coping mechanisms. Something about the practices the intervention taught—increasing sensitivity to kids' cues, reflection on parenting, and verbal responsivity—took pressure off participants. I'm not saying it's a cure-all, but it's comforting to know that a steady stream of thoughtful parent-child interactions can soothe your nerves a bit.

It's wise to talk about parenting stress in the context of early language and literacy learning because, while relative stress ebbs and flows, research suggests that a steep incline typically takes place in the earliest years, as kids grow from infants to toddlers. Theorists attribute this to the intensity of wrangling kids as they get more mobile, vocal, and autonomous. After that point, parenting stress seems to hold pretty steady, natural disasters and catastrophes aside.

Stress is obviously major for families experiencing homelessness, intimate-partner violence, job insecurity, and other major upheavals. But the subtler accumulation of minor stressors—the daily hassles of parenting—are important determinants of parent well-being, parent-child interactions, and child educational outcomes, too. (And, to be clear, *daily hassles* is a technical term. I've never felt more *seen* than the day I discovered the Parenting Daily Hassles Intensity Scale in the *Journal of Marriage and Family*. The struggle, ample documentation shows, *is* real.) Routine parenting work, like feeding picky eaters, managing stockpiles of family laundry, and defusing temper tantrums, can compound into distress, depending upon how frequent and intense the demands and how proximal and dense our networks of support are.

Learning how to talk to and engage with your child doesn't begin to address the financial woes, job strain, time pressure, and million other challenges real families navigate, of course. But a bit of support in building (and trusting) your capacity to nurture their cognitive, social, and emotional development can lighten your load.

———

A global team of scientists reviewing data from a vast network of GPS monitoring systems discovered in retrospect something they'd never seen before—a gentle rocking of the earth, a "wobble," they termed it, in the months that preceded a magnitude-9 earthquake in Japan. It was caused by one of the planet's tectonic plates sliding beneath another one, jamming and tearing the earth, preparing to quake. The signs were there, but no one was looking.

Like an unnoticed wobble before an earthquake, weaknesses in early-language environments are vast yet slow-moving. They pose quiet but seismic risk to kids' long-term literacy prospects. That's why parents need to become sensors in a network aimed at noticing, and correcting for, threats to children's optimal development and literacy. We don't need the expertise of a seismologist or advanced GPS technology to get this job done. A bit of history and reading science, a lot of enthusiasm, and an openness to learning and teaching will do.

Take a long view to fully appreciate and wield your influence. Whenever you speak, you do much more than deliver a message in the moment. You are laying the groundwork for lifelong literacy.

Try This at Home
Learn to Talk

Oral-language experience is critical for reading development, but making nourishing conversation with babies and young children comes more naturally to some parents than others. So I created the **TALK Method** to help even the quietest parents find something to say while reading or spending time with kids. The next time you're with your child, challenge yourself to:

TAKE TURNS. Even preverbal infants can be dynamic conversational partners, if you let them. Pause to listen for their coos and babbles and to observe their eye movements or facial expressions. When you notice their gaze and utterances, conversation gets much easier because you're responding to their prompts versus initiating talk all on your own. Acknowledge the interests and attention the child shows: *Yes, I hear you. I think the dog is pretty silly, too.* Your reply fuels early brain development.

ASK QUESTIONS. Want to give babies a language boost, even before they start talking? Try asking questions about a scene unfolding in real life or within the pages of a book you're reading, like *What's that? Do you see the bird?* or just *Ready to turn the page?* A study found that the number of questions moms asked during shared book reading with 10-month-old infants predicted language skills 8 months later.

LABEL AND POINT. There's plenty to be said for describing your surroundings or what's on a book page, as well. Pointing to everyday objects or book illustrations and talking about their colors and shapes, or discussing related action, is conversation, too. And the finger-to-page or finger-to-object connection helps bring the baby's attention in line with yours. For example, you could say, *There's the umbrella. Right there.* (Pointing.)

KEEP THE CONVERSATION GOING. Look for opportunities to extend, expand, and elaborate on whatever you're talking about. For example, while reading you could bring book content into the realm of everyday life and experience by linking characters and plot to things the child has experienced. Saying something like the following builds on the book without veering too far off topic: *Look! It's raining in the picture. We saw rain outside our window, too.*

Yes, you can have a conversation with an infant who's not yet talking, and you can keep using these same prompts as they age. Taking turns, asking questions, highlighting interesting things, and discussing books never get old. Sooner than you think, your baby will turn into a toddler who points and labels on their own, and then a preschooler who discusses and shares their reactions with you, having learned from your fine example. Trust me, all of this gets easier with time, practice, and attention. One day, it'll feel second nature.

JOURNAL PROMPTS

- Describe the current language environment in your home. Who talks directly to your little one (e.g., parents, siblings, babysitters)? When does most of the talk happen? How much of the talk is directive (giving an order or instructions; e.g., *sit down*), descriptive (labeling objects or events in a book or the environment; e.g., *It's a puppy*), or inquisitive (asking them a question; e.g., *Where is the ball?*)?

- Which of the reasons to talk with your child from day one resonate with you most?

- What interferes with your ability to carry on more conversations with your little one (e.g., fatigue, distraction, stress, reticence, lack of interest)?

- What will you do differently as a result of what you've learned about back-and-forth conversation with kids?

6

Taking Turns: How to Make Conversation a Habit from Day One

Every day, in a hundred small ways, our children ask, "Do you hear me? Do you see me? Do I matter?"

—L.R. Knost

For most of my life, I've held the strong opinion that people talk too much. Among the documents I found when thumbing through files of my old assignments from my twelve years as an Akron Public Schools student in Ohio is an ode to succinctness that I wrote for an English class. In the poem, I call on people to "get to the point," "keep things simple," and—presumably for the sake of the rhyme—to avoid "dangling participles." As an adult, I live for my self-designated Writers Wednesdays, when I don't take calls or meetings and spend a full day reveling in silence.

So imagine my surprise as a quiet-craving parent to discover that all the "let them catch you reading" stuff I'd seen on blogs and in parenting magazines was not critical for raising a reader, but making lots of conversation with babies and toddlers was. If leading reading by example alone isn't a thing, I learned, parents had best use our voices to proactively bring kids' attention to print (more on that in Chapter 8) and to build the oral vocabulary they need to make sense of words on the page.

I'm not the only parent who missed the memo about sparking meaningful conversations with kids, beginning in infancy. And the point is so important that I'm devoting a whole chapter to sharing hands-on advice for instilling strong conversational rituals and routines from people who know early talk and habit formation best. Studies of kids' early-language environments show enormous differences in both the quantity and quality of talk that kids hear and produce. Parent talkativeness varies for all kinds of reasons, from our personalities, stress levels, and time demands to our beliefs about what babies understand and cultural norms about kids' proper role in conversation with adults.

All of this matters because young children tend to follow their parents' lead when it comes to how much they talk as they grow older. LENA, a national nonprofit that offers early talk technology and data-driven early-language programs, compared the average daily vocalizations for kids who had parents with an Adult Word Count (AWC) in the highest versus lowest 20th percentile. As you can see in the following graph of kids' average daily vocalizations from LENA's Natural Language Study, talkative parents have talkative little ones and taciturn parents (caregivers who say little) have taciturn kids. In Chapter 5, we explored the dramatic consequences those differences in early-language environments and early oral-language skills may have for kids' reading and learning outcomes years later.

This is the best illustration I've seen of the need for parents to say more to inspire kids to do the same. So now the crucial question is: How?

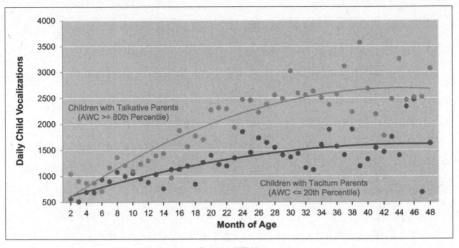

Source: LENA

The rest of this chapter offers a variety of practical strategies for improving family talk to give you a point of departure. Experiment with each to discover the methods that make you most able *and* motivated to converse more with the kids in your life.

And to the extroverts out there, you're not off the hook. You should take heed as well because parents of all stripes, from brusque to verbose, tend to overestimate how much we talk to our kids— and talking *at* kids isn't the same as talking *with* them.

Know Your Aim

When it comes to family conversation goals, you're in luck. As mentioned in Chapter 4, in 2021, LENA answered a question that's eluded researchers for decades: How much talk does it take to tilt kids' learning trajectories sky high? They found that if you're aiming for optimal brain development, then at least 40 conversational turns—back-and-forth exchanges calculated when the adult or child says something and the other responds within 5 seconds—per hour is the magic number.

The calculation was based on a 10-year longitudinal study that showed that kids who engaged in a greater number of conversational turns between 18 and 24 months old had higher IQs in middle school.

Indeed, the quest to determine what matters most in early-language environments has taken major leaps from earlier days, when researchers huddled in homes recording family chatter and then transcribed and coded the data by hand (for years!) to discern patterns.

Jill Gilkerson, the chief research and evaluation officer at LENA, has been a part of the effort for twenty years and still remembers the sparse lavender web page featuring a six-sentence job description that wooed her to the organization. She defended her dissertation as a PhD candidate in the UCLA Department of Linguistics on a Friday in Los Angeles and started work at the Boulder, Colorado, nonprofit on Monday.

The start-up had two employees and no technology at that point. But the mission to build a "talk pedometer" that could count words in a child's natural environment, document all kinds of linguistic behaviors, and expand the frontiers of language knowledge was enticement enough. Her years of study had underscored that a whole lot of theory in linguistics was based on precious little data—and she wanted to change that.

Gilkerson says that collecting data to contribute to academic study intrigued her at first, but that over time she's come to value that data most as a tool to directly improve kids' lives. "I'm super interested and motivated by the fact that we can measure something important that we couldn't do before, and that we can actually give that information to parents," she told me. "It really does motivate

behavior change and it does help the children. We're able to demonstrate that empirically, which is pretty cool."

At the time she started, though, the very notion of recording
babies' lives at home and giving parents feedback was greeted with
derision as often as it was with enthusiasm within the research community, she recalls. *It's too noisy,* many in the field protested. *How
could you distinguish speech from digestive noises or crying? What parent wants researchers listening in on them all day?*

Despite the skepticism, a growing team of LENA researchers and
engineers persisted to create recording technology and software that
separates talk from other vocalizations, allows for the recording of
up to 16 hours of continuous speech data, and allows for customized
analysis down to the millisecond. And *thousands* of parents have
raised their hands to have researchers capture and analyze the conversations their kids are party to at home and in childcare settings.

More than 10,000 children from birth to age 3 have donned tiny
LENA recorders in the front pockets of special biblike vests. Their
data has been uploaded to the cloud, analyzed by LENA software,
and reported back to researchers, parents, and early-childcare centers. The expert analysis has yielded tremendous insight into the
quality and quantity of talk kids need.

For example, the research shows that high-talk parents aren't
talking nonstop from sunup to sundown as you might imagine.
Rather, they have short 5-minute bursts of dynamic conversation
more frequently than the rest of us. Parents who were at 40 turns or
more per hour on average for their entire reporting day had peaks
and valleys of talk across the day, meeting or exceeding the 40-turn
threshold for only about 8 hours. And even within those hours talk
ebbed and flowed noticeably.

"It was down to about half of that hour where they're having that more intensive back-and-forth," Gilkerson explained to me. "So, on average it came out to about 25 minutes. It's basically five five-minute sessions throughout that hour. And during those five minutes, it's just two turns during each minute."

The good news is, you don't have to break out a stopwatch to ensure that you're on track. "Just if you're focused on your child and you can get one turn, try to get one more," Gilkerson advises. "If you've done that, then you've got your two in that minute and that's a great thing. That's going to set you on the road to making this more of a habit, getting the child used to talking, getting you used to talking. And that will just blossom from there."

Remind Yourself

Most of us don't have access to LENA technology to count the words we exchange with our children and give us personalized feedback reports. Still, we can all benefit from the knowledge that the vast majority of parents could stand to talk a lot more. I asked B. J. Fogg, a Stanford University professor and habit expert, how parents might ingrain better conversational routines and patterns in everyday life when we don't have access to cutting-edge monitoring and feedback. He assured me that measurement is "helpful, but not essential."

A count of words or conversational turns can raise parents' awareness of how little they talk to their children, help them understand the gap, and motivate them to make changes. But we don't need personalized data to uphold good talk habits. Sticking with a desired behavior over time requires something else, Fogg said—well-chosen reminder prompts to take the specific language-boosting actions that we're after. As he writes in his book *Tiny Habits*, "No prompt no action."

So, what would a set of habits designed to increase the quality or quantity of talk look like, and what kinds of prompts could trigger them? Good habit options would be anything that encourages us to TALK (take turns, ask questions, label and point, and keep the conversation going), as described in Chapter 5. And as for the prompts we use to remind us to build those habits, the more specific the trigger, the better. Fogg recommends identifying a particular moment in your daily schedule and formulating a commitment, such as "After I [EVENT], I will [TARGET ACTION]."

Cooking with Fogg's recipe, I came up with the following ideas for prompting more and better parent-child talk. Look them over and see if some would work for you.

GENERAL
- After I hear my baby coo or babble, I will respond in a complete sentence.
- After my child points or gestures, I will look in the direction of interest.

MEALTIMES
- After I sit down for breakfast, I will read a daily meditation aloud.
- After we sit down for dinner, I will say a short prayer or expression of gratitude.

DIAPER CHANGES
- After I pick up the baby wipes, I will sing a nursery rhyme.
- After I fasten the diaper, I will describe an item in the room.

BATHING

- After I turn off the faucet, I will count down out loud: *5-4-3-2-1, bath time!*
- After I dry the baby off, I will describe the outfit I'm going to put on them.

NAPTIME OR BEDTIME

- After I swaddle my baby, I will sing a lullaby.
- After my baby wakes up, I will count their fingers and toes aloud.

IN TRANSIT

- After we walk out the front door, I will say, "What a [sunny/cloudy/rainy] day."
- After I fasten the seat belt, I will say, "We're on our way to [destination]."

STORYTIME

- After I pick up a book, I will describe the cover illustration.
- After I close a book, I will share what I liked most about it.

Importantly, I pegged these habits to some of the most precise, reliable occurrences I could imagine. Not eating, sleeping, diaper changes, and errand-running in general, but the tiny moments that punctuate long days with littles—sitting down to a meal, picking up baby wipes, fastening a seat belt.

Think through the details of your day and identify specific opportunities to TALK like those just described. Then go a step further and write down ways that you could remind yourself to take the targeted actions in the first place. For example, you could post a parent-talk tip sheet on your refrigerator or leave it on the coffee table in the living room, if you won't overlook it in the hubbub of daily life. Even better are super-specific reminders, such as a bookmark in your baby's book bin featuring a few questions to ask during a read-aloud, or a changing pad cover with a nursery rhyme toile design to remind you to sing during diaper duty. You'll get to a point where the talking, rhyming, and question-asking are second nature, but nothing beats a good prompt in the beginning.

And while specific environmental cues like those described are ideal, I also advocate using technology to keep back-and-forth dialogue top of mind. For big-picture reminders, follow baby/toddler/preschooler-focused social media accounts that emphasize the habits you're trying to instill to infuse some purpose into your scroll time. Viral videos of kids interacting with caregivers often provide excellent models of parents noticing kids' cues, following their interests, and encouraging talk. This kind of inspiration can keep us motivated and on track in moments when we might otherwise be distracted.

Also, try creating your own text, email, or calendar reminders as well, to see what works for you. This could be an automated text at the end of your workday reminding you to share a story or joke with your little one or a pre-dinner notification telling you to put your device away and focus on family while you dine. Don't expect to find the perfect prompt right away. Plan to experiment.

For example, when I moved to a new house with early-morning trash and recycling collection on Tuesdays, I couldn't for the life of me remember to move our bins out of the shed at the right time. I put it on my digital calendar only to notice it after I was at work. I wrote it on a physical calendar in the kitchen that I never consult.

I set up a recurring email reminder, which I also never noticed at an opportune time. Finally, I used an SMS scheduling app to send myself a recurring text message every Tuesday at 7 a.m. It has worked like a charm because the text arrives just as I'm headed out the door to walk with my daughter to her bus stop. I either drag the bins out on the way to the stop or when I'm walking back afterward.

When summertime rolls around, I may need a new prompt because I'll no longer be escorting my daughter to the bus stop. Or perhaps the habit will be instilled by then. No cue required.

What's a just-in-time reminder for you? Would a Post-it note on your dashboard be enough to trigger some wordplay in the car, or would it fade into the background and be ignored? Would a stack of TableTopics cards on your kitchen table invite discussion? The prompts each of us needs are as unique as we are, so experiment until you find some that work for you now.

Follow the Child's Lead

Notes to self are great, but your child is the ultimate reminder system. Tune in to their speech, from coo to babble to word, and respond in kind, preferably within 5 seconds, and you'll never have to set an alarm or mark your calendar to talk it up.

Araceli Diaz, the vice president of education for the Concilio, a nonprofit serving Latino families in North Texas that's been a LENA Start partner since 2018, says that getting in the habit of "just following what our children are doing and engaging" is the key. And she's not just spouting program talking points; she was living it firsthand. When I spoke to her, she was overseeing the initiative—and taking part as a parent participant.

Even though she had long been aware of the benefits of early language, she said her first report showed that her conversational turns count wasn't even in the 50th percentile. Like so many of us, she'd overestimated how much she talked to her baby.

The LENA Start parent program includes lessons and personalized feedback on conversation dynamics and TV/electronic sound in the home, based on the family's talk pedometer recordings. She credits these with sparking aha moments for parents (herself included), where they think, *I can have these conversations with my child, with my baby, and even though they're not speaking, necessarily, they're connecting with me, they're seeing their parents talk to them.*

For example, in one LENA Start lesson, parents are taught to use mealtimes to build vocabulary and grow kids' brains. There's so much more that parents can say beyond "Here comes the airplane" as they weave a spoon of mush through the air toward a baby's mouth. LENA encourages parents to talk about the names of food and drinks; categories like fruits, vegetables, and meats; and the utensils and cooking tools they use to prepare and deliver the food. The curriculum also serves up descriptive words to help parents delve into the taste, temperature, texture, colors, size, shape, and quantity of the foods on hand. That's along with action words to describe the biting, chewing, and swallowing that happens at the table, plus phrases like *please* and *thank you* that bring courtesy into play.

Following the child, in this setting, might be noticing them watching you spoon peas onto a plate and saying, *We need more peas on the plate—one, two, three spoonfuls for you!* Or, if they turn toward a pan of stir-fry, saying, *Yes, the vegetables are cooking. Do you hear the sizzle? It sounds like sssss.*

Seen this way, most anything a child vocalizes or does can be taken as a talking prompt. Diaz says when she sees her daughter playing independently, she uses that as a nudge to jump in and say, "Hey, what are you playing with? What are these colors?"

With or without a talk pedometer, parents can provide kids with the language nutrition they need and learn to see kids' talk—and even their silence—as calls to conversation.

Limit Kids' Media Use

Sometimes the secret to doing more of one thing is doing less of another. Such is the case with positive, responsive parent-child interactions and kids' media use. If you want to talk more (and more dynamically), limiting the time your child spends glued to a screen is a great place to start.

There was a time when parents only had to contend with television at home, but today smartphones and tablets make media accessible everywhere and at any time. An analysis of data from parent time diaries, which is more accurate than estimates parents give in surveys, found that average daily screen time for kids younger than 2 years old more than doubled from 1.32 hours in 1997 to 3.05 hours in 2014. I suspect it's even higher today, given the ways the pandemic disrupted work-home separation, as well as childcare and school accessibility.

As often as we can, we should provide the specific, tailored responses to kids' utterances that they need to grow vocabulary and understanding. Our words beat the unresponsive drone of the television or YouTube every time. Unlike older children, toddlers struggle to learn from video—even live video—without someone physically present alongside them to signal that the video content is useful and worth paying attention to.

Indeed, LENA data shows a negative correlation between hours of television and other electronic media detected in recordings and language ability in young children. And a longitudinal study of 2,441 Canadian children found that higher levels of screen time at 24 and 36 months old were associated with worse performance on developmental screenings at 36 and 60 months old, respectively.

For kids under 2 years old, the American Academy of Pediatrics guidelines recommend very limited media use, and only when an adult is alongside the child to "co-view, talk, and teach," say, when parent and child are video chatting with out-of-town grandparents. That is, media use for the youngest kids should be brief, interactive, and supervised to benefit little ones. Many parents don't want to hear this, because digital devices have become an integral part of our lives, but the research is clear: showing a baby videos on your phone is not educational.

Once kids reach preschool age, the time they spend on devices should continue to be in the company of an adult and limited to minutes, not hours, per day. On average, one study found that American preschool-aged kids spend approximately *4 hours per day* exposed to screens at home and in childcare. That's four times the American Academy of Pediatrics' recommendation for the age group.

The bright side is: once kids are 3 years old, there is evidence that they can gain valuable alphabetic knowledge from educational media, such as the public television shows *Sesame Street* and *Super Why!*, especially if a parent watches alongside them, discusses, and elaborates on the content. So there comes a time when co-viewing video content can create opportunities to talk, build vocabulary, and support kids' development.

And you don't have to commit to watching every episode of *Daniel Tiger* to fulfill your parental obligations. A rule of thumb is to watch the first few episodes to gauge the quality and appropriateness of a show for your child and model how to engage with its content. Once you've set the tone and shown them how media works, then you can slip away from future episodes to tackle other tasks or take a break.

Preschooler media use is particularly prevalent in households with multiple children because parents use smartphones or tablets to quiet or separate bickering siblings. But researchers warn that the quick fix has lasting consequences: "the negative impact brought by excessive screen time will actually increase the burden for parents in later life." That's because, as the researchers found, each additional hour of screen-time exposure is associated with kids' increased risk for emotional, behavioral, social, and attentional problems down the line.

One strategy that works for many families is drawing hard boundaries around screen use, such as having device-free dinners; setting screen curfews, after which all devices are docked, charging, and unavailable for use; or creating screen-free rooms or zones at home. Thousands of families have signed on for Screen-Free Saturdays, a nonprofit initiative that promotes unplugging, recharging, and disconnecting from the incessant marketing and manipulations of media and technology companies. You could give it a try and make it an event by powering down devices at sundown on Friday, getting a great night's rest, and fueling a day of family fun and conversation on Saturday.

Put Your Own Phone Down

Parents' own use of media also adversely affects family talk. Numerous studies have found that when parents are on their phones, they're less engaged with and responsive to kids—verbally and nonverbally—sometimes even leading to injury when kids engage in risky bids for attention.

Now, I'm not saying we have to give up Netflix and devote our full attention to our children every waking second. But let's be honest about where our focus is, what that focus means, and how we might take more opportunities to unplug from devices and tune in to our kids. A survey of 2,000 parents of school-aged children revealed:

- 69 percent felt "addicted" to their phone
- 62 percent admitted to spending too much time on their cell phones when they were with their kids
- 50 percent had been asked by their child to put their phone away

Knowing better and doing better are two different things. Breaking our bad phone habits often requires serious intervention—mindfulness intervention, that is. Jon Kabat-Zinn has defined mindfulness as "paying attention in a particular way: on purpose, in the present moment, and nonjudgmentally." Practically speaking, mindfulness is the ability to create mental and emotional space between a stimulus and our response. It's cultivating the awareness, self-regulation, and perspective to consciously choose our words and actions (or silence and inaction) in the moment.

In the past decade numerous studies have investigated mindful parenting and found evidence that it can reduce caregiver stress and coparenting disagreements. Some of the same techniques that have helped parents step out of autopilot and respond to kids more skillfully can also serve to help us set aside our phones and converse more in person. Consider that mindfulness-based approaches have helped people battling phone addictions in other contexts. In a pilot study of phone-obsessed university students, mindfulness-based training was associated with a reduction in the students' cravings for their smartphones and in their smartphone use time.

An easy way for parents to curb device use is to make a mindfulness practice out of the phone itself. We can follow the example of Marta Brzosko of the Self-Awareness Blog, who "created room for more conscious decision-making" around her phone by taking ten mindful breaths whenever the urge to reach for it emerged.

Similarly, clinical psychologist Mitch Abblett recommends that after we reach for our phones we pause and sit with our devices in hand. Let our thumbs hover over the screen. Take a full, deep breath into the belly and notice whatever thoughts, physical sensations, or emotions arise. Get curious about it all, note whatever feelings come up, and continue to return to attending to the breath.

"We simply (and yet with great difficulty) need to learn to hold our technology more lightly—with more awareness," Abblett explained in a *Mindful* magazine article. "Consider making your phone itself a cue for waking up instead of checking out."

Reward Yourself

Now that technology has allowed us to see the child's language experience from the child's vantage point, we can better appreciate our influence. Think of your own child and the impact you can make for them over a lifetime, and applaud yourself for what you've read, said, and done to bolster their literacy thus far. That's all part of a winning early-literacy formula.

Maybe there was a particularly talkative hour this week or a day with less TV than usual—and that's amazing. No one gets better at this by beating ourselves up about our shortcomings. We get better by finding the good, making it regular, and being thoughtful about adding other positive habits to the mix one by one.

Applaud yourself anytime you notice that you've paid loving attention to your child, responded with brain-building language, sung the nursery rhyme, narrated the activity, turned off the TV, or followed their gaze. Affirmation of the good you've done, when you catch yourself doing it, will do more to cement the habit than dwelling on missteps ever could. It could be a silent fist pump or a whispered *Good job, Mom*. Whatever real-time positive reinforcement resonates with you will wire in the new habit like nothing else.

In fact, Fogg recommends celebrating your habit three times when you're in the early days of forming it—right when you remember to do it, while you're doing it, and immediately after. Bing. Bang. Boom!

"Emotions create habits," he states. "Not repetition. Not frequency. Not fairy dust. Emotions." So go ahead, get in your feelings about any baby steps you take toward becoming a more nurturing, responsive, brain-building caregiver. You deserve it, and your baby does, too.

Try This at Home
Play Every Day

Fun, social interactions (aka play!) start in infancy and have positive impacts for both parent and child. A study of naturally occurring baby games, like peekaboo—where a parent and child share attention, gazes, facial expressions, touches, gestures, and vocalizations—showed that they were associated with a boost in the release of the feel-good hormone oxytocin.

In your child's early years, it's great to have a few go-to games in your toolkit for times when you need a conversational pick-me-up. Boost your talk and playfulness anytime, anywhere by keeping some language-rich games in your metaphorical back pocket.

I SPY ages incredibly well—with variations for babies, toddlers, and preschoolers—works in a variety of settings, and requires no assembly.

The game uses the phrase "I spy with my little eye something _____" to set up a hunt for an object of your choice. Start by choosing an object—say, a blue dictionary on the kitchen counter—and then give hints: *I spy with my little eye something blue.* The child looks around and (hopefully!) responds by saying they see a blue book or perhaps simply pointing. Then your child takes a turn to give you hints to find the objects they choose, giving them a wonderful chance to flex their expressive vocabulary muscles.

As your child grows, you can adapt the game to pose new challenges. With the youngest children, you might use it to draw attention to colors or shapes. Later you can amp it up to direct your child toward certain letters or rhyming words, as in "I spy something that rhymes with *car.* Yes, the peanut butter jar!" The possibilities are endless, but here are a few to get you started:

- Shapes: *I spy something that's square.*
- Colors: *I spy something red.*
- Letters: *I spy the letter T.*
- Letter sounds: *I spy the letter that says /s/.*
- Rhyming: *I spy something that rhymes with* stair.

- Onsets and rimes: *I spy something that starts with the /k/ sound.*
- Ending sounds: *I spy something that ends with the /r/ sound.*

JOURNAL PROMPTS

- What are some habits you can establish to support more back-and-forth conversation with your child?

- What daily occurrences (e.g., mealtimes, bath times, naptimes, etc.) can you use to help you establish those habits?

- What actions will you take now to support those habits, such as placing books or talking points in prominent locations at home?

7

Sound Instruction: The Tenor
of Reading Success

*Everything in writing begins with language. Language
begins with listening.*

—Jeanette Winterson

In the 1960s, listeners from Los Angeles to London were charmed
by Shirley Ellis and her catchy tunes. Archival footage shows her
poised in dazzling gowns cinched at the waist just so, the vigor and
verve of her vocals holding audiences rapt.

The Congress Recordings songstress had a single on the Billboard
Hot Rhythm and Blues Top 10 list in January 1965, alongside the
Temptations' "My Girl," Marvin Gaye's "How Sweet It Is (to Be
Loved by You)," the Supremes' "Come See about Me," and Sam
Cooke's "A Change Is Gonna Come." Her hit still resounds, although
Ellis is too often regarded as an American music history footnote, not
a legend like those contemporaries.

The song, inspired by a rhyming game she played as a child, has
stayed in rotation through the years in television, movies, commer-
cials, and cover versions. Runway models walked to its rhythms in a
Stella McCartney fashion show to rave reviews from *Women's Wear*

Daily the same year that a major retailer's commercial featured a family singing it on a road trip. Howard Stern says singing the ditty is his "schtick with kids." Jessica Lange performed a show-stopping rendition on *American Horror Story* that catapulted the oldie-but-goodie to meme status on TikTok. And the song's title continues to be invoked as a tortured metaphor for trade articles about everything from corporate rebranding efforts to the merits of monogramming.

Yes, "The Name Game" endures. Odds are you know the tune. Something in its rhythm and rules—remove the first consonant of a name; replace it with a B, F, or M; then add a *bo, fo, fee, fi,* or *mo* in the designated spots—keeps the song humming along. Despite prognostications that it was a "novelty tune" destined to disappear when the freshness of its nonsensical humor wore off, it lives on. The inventive wordplay and nods to the hand-clapping, jump-roping culture of black girlhood also won Ellis credit for ushering in a new form of American music. Her picture is *the* image in an encyclopedia entry documenting "proto-rap," the pre-1980s stylistic forebear to hip-hop's beats, rhymes, and banter. I'd argue that she's also a standard-bearer for another movement that she scarcely could have anticipated—early support for *phonological awareness.*

Let's get down to the nitty-gritty.

Phonological Awareness Defined

Phonological awareness is right up there with oral language and letter knowledge as a pillar of literacy. This umbrella concept encompasses consciousness of a range of sound units within words, including syllables, onsets, rimes, and phonemes. (If you're thinking, *Huh?,* don't worry: definitions coming up.)

Syllables are pronunciation units that include a vowel sound and optional consonant sounds before and/or after the vowel. For example, the word *soccer* has two syllables. However, the definition isn't as clear-cut as you might think. Does *bottling* have two syllables or three? Does *Worcestershire* have two, three, or four? Well, it depends on who's talking, where they're from, and who's counting.

An *onset* is the initial consonant or consonant cluster sound in a word—the /t/ sound in *team*, for example, or the /sp/ sound in *spoon*. Some words, like *air,* do not have an onset. The *rime* unit (fraternal twin to *rhyme*) is the vowel sound and any consonant sounds that follow. For example, the "eam" in *team. Phonemes* (e.g., /t/, /ē/, or /m/) are the smallest speech-sound units of them all. In English, there are forty-four.

As you probably gathered from the example, *team* is spelled with four letters but has only three phonemes. By contrast, *tax* is spelled with three letters but has four phonemes: /t/, /a/, /k/, and /s/.

Parents can think of each level of phonological awareness as a finer- and finer-grained presentation of the same basic skill. Sound knowledge generally proceeds from larger linguistic units (e.g., syllables) to smaller ones (e.g., phonemes). A child would usually recognize that *breakfast* has two syllables before grasping that it starts with a /b/ sound or that it has eight sounds in all—/b/, /r/, /e/, /k/, /f/, /i/, /s/, and /t/.

It's not a strict stage-by-stage progression, though. Little ones don't have to master syllables before they can grapple with rhyming words or discern individual speech sounds. In day-to-day life, kids are exposed to the phonological structure of the language, at all the levels at once, anytime words are spoken. Their knowledge of certain units develops and consolidates faster than others, influenced by their innate abilities, the language(s) they learn, the songs they sing, the books they read, and other language experiences.

Parents don't need to follow a strict scope and sequence to impart these skills. Everyday life provides plenty of opportunities to sing nursery rhymes and play with sounds. You don't need to worry about spending a set amount of time on one element of phonological awareness versus another. Just be aware that the ability to discern and manipulate speech sounds takes time to develop, so it makes sense to emphasize certain skills at certain points in your child's development.

For example, focus on syllable-blending (*bat* plus *man* equals *batman*) and syllable-clapping activities with 2- and 3-year-olds. For 3- and 4-year-olds, emphasize rhyming skills and initial letter-sound comparisons (*What happens if I turn the /k/ sound in* cat *into a /b/ sound?*). With 4- and 5-year-olds, dig into individual sounds. By ages 5 and 6, they can be initiating sound games on their own, by doing things like talking in Pig Latin to friends. Oday ouyay ememberray atthay amegay?

While all the phonological skills are important and interrelated, phoneme awareness—knowledge of individual sounds—packs the most punch, says Gail Gillon, director of the University of Canterbury Child Well-Being Research Institute. "What is predictive of reading success is being aware of the individual sounds in words—so phoneme awareness, not necessarily rhyme awareness or syllable awareness or word-level awareness," she explains. "I do say to parents that lots of rhyming stories are a great introduction, but you need to move to getting even young children to really tune into the first sounds as the starting point. It needs to move to that phoneme level because particularly as they get towards school age, they need to start listening to the first sounds in words."

Knowing that these sound-discernment skills are all located along a single continuum gives parents important insight into how their child is progressing on the road to literacy, says Jason Anthony, a professor at the University of South Florida who specializes in language and literacy acquisition. In general, children who do well at these things early on are going to continue to do well and learn to read without difficulty. "The reason it's important to understand that all of these things fall under phonological awareness is that you can actually play with your child, do these sound activities, and encourage their literacy development long before they ever reach formal reading instruction," he explains.

It also means that the professionals can identify early which kids are likely to have more difficulty. "We don't have to wait until third grade to decide, 'This child is failing school, he can't read,'" Anthony explains. "Now we're in a much better place to identify a child at risk of reading failure at kindergarten entry or even preschool, not with perfect accuracy, of course, but we're in a much better place to do that."

How to Teach Phonological Awareness

Whatever urgency or anxiety you feel about raising a reader needs to be held at a distance during the actual work. In fact, to the greatest extent possible, building phonological awareness needs to look, talk, walk, and act like *play*.

It's not drill and kill. It's singing "The Name Game." It's talking in Pig Latin. It's playing I Spy with beginning sounds or rhyming words instead of colors. (*I spy something that rhymes with* tike. *Yes, the bike!*)

When you recite nursery rhymes, you're heightening kids' sensitivity to the syllables and the beginning, middle, and ending sounds within words. The stress patterns of classics like "Jack and Jill Went up the Hill" help them learn about syllables and rhymes, important phonological awareness skills. And the alliteration in a rhyme like "Peter Piper Picked a Peck of Pickled Peppers" accentuates the /p/ sound and distinguishes it from surrounding sounds, a finer-grained level of phoneme sensitivity.

Spoonerisms are another fun source of phonological play. Sometimes they occur naturally in conversation when you accidentally say things like I "zipped the skoom meeting" instead of "I skipped the Zoom meeting." But you can intentionally mix up initial sounds as a game, and get your little one in on the action. You could explain the game and give examples, by saying: *Let's mix up some sounds. Instead of saying, "It's dinnertime," we can say, "It's tinnerdime" if we flip-flop the starting sounds. What happens if you swap the starting sounds in "Tootsie Roll"? Yes, that would be "rootsie toll"!*

The lesson from all this is that you can easily build phonological awareness anytime, anywhere, with just your voice and your child's attention. You don't need a book (although they can help). You don't need paper. You don't need a table. You don't even need to be still— neighborhood strolls or car, bus, or subway rides present lovely opportunities for this kind of banter.

So much of what we associate with learning is informed by what we experienced in our own schools. But teaching needn't look like a formal classroom with a parent at a whiteboard and the child behind a desk (or computer). Family teaching at home and on the go should be much more organic than that, and when it comes to phonological awareness, at least, it can definitely be fun and on the fly.

You can spark practice just by asking questions:

- *How many words can you think of that rhyme with* in? *What are they?* **win, bin, kin, sin, thin**

- *What sound does* car *start with?* **/k/**
- *What sounds do you hear in the word* bat? **/b/, /a/, /t/**
- *What's the word* homework *without* home? **work**
- *Here's your bag. Change the /b/ sound to an /s/ sound. What's the new word?* **sag**
- *What word can I make from the sounds /y/, /e/, /s/?* **Yes!**

Pro tip: leave out the word *and* when you are listing sounds to make your point clearer and more easily understood by your little listener.

Be relaxed in your approach and mix up the levels where you focus attention—syllable, first or ending sounds, or individual sounds. Even within levels there are opportunities to keep things fresh when you focus on blending sounds, segmenting, deleting, and swapping them. Just remember: Keep. It. Light. It's wordplay, not an interrogation! Get excited and cheer together when your child solves the puzzle.

A great irony of raising readers is that the critically important, life-trajectory-altering, high-stakes work of building these foundational skills is best done with the lightest, nearly imperceptible touch. The subtler the accumulation of moments of speech, song, and play over the course of years, the better, experts agree.

That said, research reveals a couple of effective strategies that *do* require a little advance prep: namely, using visuals to teach sound segmentation. "Auditory imagery" is in fact thought to be part of how the brain processes language. One study provided evidence that training beginning readers with pictures of the mouth positions associated with different sounds (e.g., lips closed for /p/ and lips rounded and open for /o/) helped the learners read words more easily. The brain's representation of a sound is thought to be influenced by both acoustic cues and by the vocal tract gestures (e.g., round of the lips) that are used to produce speech, so the dual approach may help letter sounds stick in memory. Likewise, another study provided evidence that training struggling readers with images of an object whose name starts with the target letter's sound and whose shape includes the target letter as a salient visual feature boosted their learning of letter-sound associations. So those alphabet posters with snakes in S shapes are on to something.

Hand-making materials like this can bring an element of personality and care into lessons, so try sketching out some objects in the shape of their starting letter. It can get silly and that's fine—it's also memorable and engaging. Alternatively, you could snag a copy of *Itchy's Alphabet*, a multisensory sound-learning book that illustrates the letters and accompanying objects.

You may have noticed that my discussion of phonological awareness slid into talk of teaching letter sounds. In real life, you're going to be teaching many skills simultaneously, and research supports that approach. Spellings, pronunciations, and meaning are all intertwined in learning and memory. "As scientists and researchers, we always want to separate everything and analyze everything. Take it all down to all its little pieces and study each little piece—and there's value in that," Anthony says. "But what we've also found is that there's a lot of value in teaching these things concurrently."

Books come in handy for other levels of phonological awareness, too. *Faint Frogs Feeling Feverish: And Other Terrifically Tantalizing Tongue Twisters* by Lilian Obligado works wonders to help your child grasp initial phonemes. And your classic rhyming books are always fun to read and share.

Whichever approach you take (wordplay, books, visual cues, etc.), remember to keep it fun and be encouraging. "If you're trying to do exercise and it's really tough and you've got a trainer or someone telling you you're not getting it right, you just stop going," Gillon from the University of Canterbury says. "And it's the same with children. They like to do things that they're getting lots of positive praise and encouragement for. If it's fun, they'll keep doing it."

Or, put another way, *if it's not fun, don't do it.*

Once elementary school literacy instruction begins, you can lay off the sound awareness practice altogether unless your child has a known issue. Their phonemic awareness will continue to develop without special emphasis as they're explicitly taught letter sounds and decoding strategies. In this new phase, you can explore other language and literature opportunities together.

Home Language Advantage

Parents who speak languages other than English at home may worry about whether they are pronouncing English phonemes correctly, and they can be hesitant to work on phonological awareness as a result. Don't even worry about it. There's evidence to suggest that phonological awareness originally developed in a different language—like the parent and child's first language—transfers to phonological awareness and improves word-reading skills in English. All languages have underlying sound structures that children need to gain familiarity with, so there's value in working on phonological awareness in whatever language the parent or caregiver is most comfortable with. Take pride in your first language, keep it central to your child's life, and seize opportunities for wordplay. You can make up silly sentences with words beginning with the same sound in Spanish or another language just as easily as in English.

"Particularly for parents of young children that might be struggling themselves with learning a language or English might not be their first language, they worry sometimes, 'Should I be just trying to speak English?'" Gillon explains. "I'm saying the opposite: No. Use your own language that you're confident in when they're little, and get them to hear the sounds in your home language and develop those skills, because that's an absolute treasure."

There's beauty and consequence in using your own language, she says. "It's important for little ones that they just start hearing the sounds in their language—being consciously aware of the first sounds and words, listening for the rhythm of their language, and really bringing their attention to the sound structure of their language."

Early on, kids are developing the cognitive ability to hear sounds in words, starting with listening to the rhythms of songs and every-day language. So even if it's a goal for your child to learn English, in this early stage there's a benefit to using your home language to build phonological skill. There's evidence for cross-language transfer.

"It's not necessarily a direct transfer for all languages, because it does depend on the different languages you are learning, but it's certainly helpful," Gillon adds. "If you're good at phonological awareness in your first language, you will pick up those same types of phonological awareness skills when you come to learn a second language. And equally, if you struggle in one language, you will struggle in another."

But don't stop there. If English fluency is your goal, seek out opportunities for your child to gain exposure to English phonemes, the English alphabet, and oral language. The research is still accu-mulating, but there's an emerging case that phonological awareness in a second language is heavily influenced by oral-language ability in that language and how different the first and second languages

are from each other. The stronger a child's overall language experience in both, the better.

To my earlier point about parent power: you don't have to provide all the language experience your child needs yourself. You can
give them the best of what you have and seek out what you can't
directly provide. Sometimes, the conversation partners, word-game
players, and nursery-rhyme singers you need may be found in friends
or family members who speak the target language, at library programs, or in early-childcare centers. Audiobooks, recorded music,
and cartoons in the second language provide language exposure, too
(albeit without the total benefits of a live human providing contingent responses). Get clear on what you can give, and get intentional
about supplementing the rest.

Accentuate the Differences

Even native English-speaking parents worry that their regional, cultural, or ethnic accents or dialect may hinder their ability to teach a
child the sounds of "standard" English. These are complex, weighty
issues. Sometimes racially and linguistically marginalized kids grow
up to be teachers who question their own grasp of the language.

Marcelle Haddix, distinguished dean's professor of literacy, race,
and justice at Syracuse University, had a student in her undergradu-
ate literacy methods class ask, "How can I teach reading when I
can't even pronounce the words right?" If a college student who
wanted to make a profession of teaching carried this level of doubt,
imagine how many parents—untrained and unsupported—feel.

Some dialects are more closely aligned with the English taught in
school. Others—even those that are just as complex, long-standing,
rule-governed, and legitimate—are wrongly dismissed and thought

to be a degraded version of "the standard." But every single speaker of English learns a dialect (a particular combination of grammar, vocabulary, and pronunciation), and none guarantees literacy acquisition.

In fact, respect for and exploration of dialect variations can be wonderful launching pads for language and literacy learning. "Sensitivity to dialectical differences can be taught and can be learned," Anthony says. "And there's some research that shows that individuals who can code-switch fluently may actually be at a metalinguistic advantage." Translation: people who can move between dialects or variations with ease may have better awareness of language that boosts linguistic processing and learning. The trick is to embrace and interrogate the differences, versus minimizing or ignoring them. Do your best to describe the sounds and syllables as you hear them, and point out how others might say or hear them differently.

For example, final /d/ consonants are often devoiced in African American Vernacular English (AAVE), a dialect that originated hundreds of years ago and is spoken by the majority of black elementary schoolers in the United States. That little omission of vibration of the vocal cords means that many speakers of that dialect often initially spell unconventionally, for example, writing *salat* for *salad*. Of course, all kids spell unconventionally at first for various reasons driven by their oral-language experience and knowledge of English writing. This is no different than the pronunciation variations that lead British kids to hear and spell *ticket* as *tickit* at higher rates than Australian kids who pronounce the second vowel sound differently.

This is nothing to be ashamed of or shy away from. Instead, observe and embrace the differences. Talk about them, bring attention to them, and in doing so deepen your child's language experience and pride in cultural and linguistic roots. The greater risk is depriving your little one of valuable learning opportunities because you're afraid of getting it wrong. As Anthony puts it, "It's more about just giving practice and exposure than it is being technically precise."

———

Kids leap into reading from a foundation of oral language, letter knowledge, and phonemic awareness. In an alphabetic writing system like ours, you can't read without the ability to identify individual sounds and form associations between them and letters. This is why a handbook of linguistics devotes the bulk of a section to "The Name Game." It's also why educators looking to gauge preschoolers' readiness to read may teach them the song—it gives them a sense of their ability to manipulate the sounds within words.

And so, a game from Shirley Ellis's childhood that likely helped her hone her own reading skills is immortalized in music, pop culture, and early literacy. Even if she's no household name, her impact is undeniable.

Try This at Home
Add Sights to Sounds

Phonological awareness is a critical pillar of early literacy that parents don't hear enough about and could do a lot to nurture. This chapter described several activities, from the Name Game and spoonerisms to Pig Latin and nursery rhymes, that you can use to raise your child's awareness of the sounds within words.

One pro tip for taking your efforts to the next level is to get physical by bringing objects and gestures into sound lessons.

There's something about a strong visual or tactile element in addition to the auditory dimension that helps kids grasp the sound blending and segmentation tasks at hand.

When highlighting syllables or onsets and rimes, you can put your hands in fists to illustrate different segments and bring them together to show blends. "What does putting *cup* [hold up right fist] and *cake* [hold up left fist] together make? *Cupcake*." (Bring fists together.) The same goes for segmenting the /k/ sound from the "at" in *cat*.

You have only two hands, so you'll need some other tools when tackling multisyllabic words or when you want to address individual sounds in words. Blocks, coins, or other small tokens that you have on hand can make sound tasks more concrete—and interesting. For example, you could line up four pennies to represent the different sounds heard in the word *sled*: /s/, /l/, /e/, /d/. You could say each sound slowly while pointing at the coin that represents it and then run your finger across each coin quickly as you pronounce the whole word. The physical materials help bring attention to the individual sounds.

JOURNAL PROMPTS

- What did you learn in this chapter about how the sounds within words relate to kids' reading development?

- What will your go-to sound games be?

- What reminders will you use to cue wordplay?

8

L Is for Liberation: How to Help Kids Crack the Alphabetic Code

The alphabet is an abolitionist.
If you would keep a people enslaved, refuse to teach them to read.
— **Harper's Weekly** editorial, 1867

Do you know what it takes to possess a letter? To unravel the mystery of two-dimensional scrawls on a page? To know an l from an i from a 1 from a line? To recognize an L in uppercase and lowercase, in cursive and print, in Times New Roman and Comic Sans alike?

It's a gargantuan climb for your child to learn these secrets—the letter names, their shapes, their sounds, their nature, their functions, and how they work together. Taking possession of the twenty-six letters of our alphabet is a victory, a claim to freedom and to power. Though most of us can't recall exactly how we came to know the letters intimately and automatically, the stories of those who do remember are instructive.

Take famed abolitionist Frederick Douglass. His road to reading started out forthrightly enough, when his enslaver's wife taught him the alphabet and a few short words. But this early instruction was cruelly cut short by a lesson his teacher received: that literacy and slavery were incompatible. In an autobiography, Douglass recalls his enslaver warning her that an enslaved person "should know nothing but to obey his master—to do as he is told to do . . . Now, if you teach [Douglass] how to read, there would be no keeping him. It would forever unfit him to be a slave."

Mass literacy was so threatening to enslavers that they routinely met black people's attempts at reading with whippings, amputations, and murder. Cutting the finger of the offending reader down to the first joint was common. Mississippi law made corporal punishment "not exceeding thirty-nine lashes" the price to be paid by groups of black people—enslaved or free—who dared assemble to learn reading or writing. South Carolina created stiffer and stiffer anti-literacy statutes between 1740 and 1834, eventually punishing black readers with up to fifty lashes. And even in states like Maryland where the law didn't prohibit such teaching, custom often did.

Historian Heather Andrea Williams explains how denying literacy was meant to deny enslaved people's very humanity and prolong their captivity. "Reading indicated to the world that this so-called property had a mind, and writing foretold the ability to construct an alternative narrative about bondage itself," she writes. "Literacy among slaves would expose slavery, and masters knew it."

And so Douglass heard his enslaver's tirade for what it was—a clear admission that literacy was no less than "the pathway from slavery to freedom." Thus motivated, he set out to learn to read "with high hope, and a fixed purpose, at whatever cost of trouble."

He mastered the letters S, L, F, and A from the scribblings of Baltimore shipyard carpenters who marked timber placements *starboard* or *larboard* side and *forward* or *aft*. He plied poor Irish immigrant boys with bread to get them to teach him the letters they knew. Then Douglass snuck away to scrawl the treasured letters with a lump of chalk on a board fence, brick wall, or pavement, and copied them in the spaces left in a white child's old *Webster's Spelling Book* until he knew them cold.

Literacy, starting with the recognition and naming of twenty-six letters, offered enslaved people a measure of mobility, privacy, and liberty that was as precious as life itself. Thousands of enslaved men, women, and children ventured on this dangerous, covert pursuit of the alphabet and the powerful words it made by any means they could, and an estimated 5 percent succeeded in learning to read by 1860.

Perhaps thousands more perished trying.

———

Your child's journey won't be this perilous. But make no mistake, literacy today is no less powerful a means of resistance and liberation. And there are still considerable obstacles to its attainment, especially for children who are poor, brown, or black.

Letters are the building blocks of the words that kids must learn to read, and in most U.S. schools, letter *names* are the very "language of instruction." But there's marked disparity in letter-name knowledge, a foundational skill that is incredibly influential in their academic trajectories, as children approach kindergarten. Lower-socioeconomic-status students tend to know substantially fewer letter names in preschool than higher-socioeconomic-status kids, which sets them up to struggle with decoding, spelling, and reading comprehension down the line.

Sit in on a typical kindergarten class and at some point you're likely to hear phrases such as:

- "How do you spell *cat*? C-A-T."
- "What's the first letter of that word? A!"
- "What letter makes the /m/ sound? That's right, M makes the /m/ sound."

To make sense of these questions, students need to both know the letter names and have a sense of the function that letters serve in words. Otherwise, children can't engage in the crucial conversations about reading and writing that they are meant to learn from.

Letter names give children the labels they need to connect the different manifestations of a letter in their memory—uppercase or lowercase, print or cursive, one font or another. And because many letter names bear some resemblance to their letter sounds (B says /b/, for example), little ones who have learned letter names have a tool for grasping and remembering the sounds they must learn in order to read. In fact, alphabetic knowledge is among the most robust, reliable early predictors of future reading success—and failure—that we have. It has long been established that kindergarten letter-name assessments do a better job of foretelling later reading achievement than a number of other linguistic, memory, and learning measures.

Letter-name knowledge is so critical that it's become a major target of early education in the United States. Preschool, kindergarten, and early-intervention program curricula often emphasize it, and kindergarten readiness tests assess it. And yet even the best classroom efforts offer too little too late for far too many children.

Heartbreaking research found that children from lower socioeconomic backgrounds who enrolled in a preschool program knew significantly fewer letter names at the start—and end—of preschool than their higher-socioeconomic-background peers. The two groups of children in the program, which had been rated "high quality" by the state of Ohio, showed about the same rate of growth in letter-name knowledge during their time in the program. But the children from lower socioeconomic backgrounds couldn't catch up to their peers, so the gap remained at the end of the year. The program wasn't *high enough* quality in this respect to ensure that all of the students entered kindergarten poised to thrive.

One large-scale pre-K evaluation showed that kids who had attended a high-quality preschool for an entire year recognized, on average, nine more letters than kids who had just begun preschool. Unless your child enrolls in preschool with ten uppercase letters already under their belt, that pace of learning isn't going to get the job done.

It's a challenge for teachers to devote enough time to assessing which uppercase and lowercase letters particular children don't know and then teaching those specific letters. Amid all the lessons in social skills, imaginative play, shapes, numbers, and colors, this crucial instruction gets curtailed.

As a parent, you must set your own letter-name knowledge standards—and you must set them high. Do not take your child's possession of the twenty-six letters of the alphabet for granted. Research suggests that preschoolers who can name eighteen uppercase letters and fifteen lowercase letters are well on their way to reading, and those who can't are likely to struggle. Aim for your child to know every letter name—uppercase and lowercase—by sight by the end of kindergarten, in line with the Common Core State Standards.

And there's no doubt that you can help. Teaching twenty-six

letters is well within even the busiest parents' capacity, especially if you start as soon as kids are old enough to recognize them, around 3 years old. Just point out letters, state their names and sounds, and describe their distinctive visual features—no extensive planning or elaborate lessons required, just light touches and incidental teaching in everyday life with your child.

There are countless opportunities to point out letters in the books you read or on the signs and labels you come across in your daily activities. You can pause on a neighborhood walk, gesture toward a stop sign, and say: *Look at the stop sign. S-T-O-P spells* stop. *Do you see the letter S? It curves this way and that.* (Trace an S shape in the air.) You can also whip out a sheet of paper in an idle moment, write a letter on it (say, your child's first initial or your own), and start a discussion about its features.

Some parents may object to the goal of knowing all the letters by the end of kindergarten, on the grounds that they learned their letters later in life and they read fine. The problem with that thinking is that, rightly or wrongly, U.S. elementary school standards are much higher today. Educators' expectations spiked after the signing of the No Child Left Behind Act in 2002 and the expansion of early-childhood education programs. Public school kindergarten teachers in 2010 were more than twice as likely to "strongly agree" or "agree" that kids should learn to read in kindergarten and that parents should ensure that their kids know the alphabet prior to entry, compared with their colleagues in 1998. These raised expectations were, in many instances, even "more pronounced among schools serving high percentages of low-income and non-White children." Children who don't know their letters in kindergarten are likely to struggle with classroom instruction, fall further behind peers, and experience feelings of anxiety and inadequacy.

You may worry that aspiring to these standards may be pushing kids too far too fast. There are educational traditions of high literacy achievement that don't even commence reading instruction until kids are 7 years old—such as in Waldorf schools or in Finland's public school system. But starting formal reading instruction that late makes sense only within an educational framework expressly designed to support it, which is absolutely not the case in the United States.

The main reason to build alphabetic knowledge early isn't that it's impossible for kids to learn it later, but that our current system offers insufficient support. Most of our public schools simply are not equipped to meet kids where they are. They are set up to teach particular content at particular grade levels, and if your child isn't there—good luck. Moreover, as children advance through the grades, their access to foundational reading instruction and effective intervention declines.

Simply put, parents need to prepare their children to thrive in the system we *have*. If your child is going to be traditionally schooled in the United States, be ready to navigate the customs, curriculum, and expectations found there. The good news is that any caregiver with even basic literacy, few to no materials, and just minutes a day can get them ready—with the right knowledge and approach.

Young children are completely capable of building alphabetic knowledge prior to school. And doing so with a parent, through play, games, and incidental teaching, is an effective—and enjoyable—route. If you haven't worked on alphabetic knowledge with your child, or you sense that they are "behind," according to today's standards, don't panic. Knowledge is power, and now that you're aware of what your child needs to learn, you can start where they are and help them climb.

Teaching Letter Names the Smart Way

As readers ourselves, parents often fail to grasp what a leap it is even to see letters as distinct from other images and graphics in print. To know an O from a circle or an H from a stick figure is the result of a long learning process, a slow-growing awareness of print and its properties. At first, pictures, letters, and numbers are all a bunch of 2D marks to be deciphered.

Parents with savvy and resources, though, tend to use a wide range of activities and contexts at home to build and reinforce alphabetic skills. They play with magnetic letters, point out letters on household items, read alphabet books, and talk about the letters in their child's name. In questionnaires, in-the-know parents reported using an average of *fourteen* out of eighteen different home-teaching contexts, from storybooks and shopping lists to letter blocks and flash cards, to engage kids with the alphabet. Brief teachable moments pave the way.

Unsurprisingly, the parents who reported teaching the ABCs the most frequently tended to be those with high expectations of what their kids should know before first grade. These parents had wisely linked the letter work they did with future school achievement. And you can do the same.

What you say to your children about letter shapes, names, and sounds—and when—matters. When you take responsibility for teaching your kids the alphabet before they start kindergarten, you're doing crucial work to support their later success. Speak with knowledge and intention, seize everyday moments, and structure your home and schedule to support deliberate learning. Here are a few ideas to get you started.

CALL LETTERS BY THEIR NAMES. While some people prefer to teach letter sounds before letter names, the fact of the matter is that kids need to know both—and instruction is simpler when you have unique and consistent labels. I say teach both at the same time. "Clearly, it is easier to say, 'Point to the A,' than to say, 'Point to the letter that says /æ/ (or /ä/ or /ā/ or /uh/),'" pioneering researcher Marilyn Jager Adams explains.

Think of the names as labeled buckets in which kids collect all their encounters with a letter—uppercase, lowercase, print, cursive, its various sounds, and so on. Over time and through exposure, in one's memory, "the label provides a means of bonding together all of one's experiences with a to-be-learned concept," Adams writes. "In doing so, it can only hasten the recognition of the similarities of the concept across its occurrences."

Recent research continues to provide support for using letter names. Studies suggest that letter-name knowledge benefits young children's spelling, for example—a crucial component of literacy development. And researchers have found evidence that combining letter-name training with letter-sound instruction accelerates letter-sound learning.

Parents' talk about letters and use of letter names can start at any time but becomes particularly powerful when kids are 3 years old and can focus on letters in print. At that point, they can begin to forge letter identities through repeated experience with their shapes, names, and sounds. This is a good time to start pointing out letters that are prominent in your home or neighborhood, such as on a stop sign, monogrammed item, or cereal box. Remember to play I Spy: *I spy with my little eye the letter S. It curves around like this.* (Draw an S shape in the air.) *Do you see an S?*

ASSESS LETTER-NAME KNOWLEDGE. Take care to determine which, if any, letters your child already knows. You may be surprised by the knowledge they already possess.

You can find out by writing uppercase and lowercase letters on separate index cards, showing them to the child in a random order, and asking them to name them. Be sure to record the date and whether they responded correctly or not. If the response surprises you or is noteworthy in some respect, jot that down on the back of the card as well. These casual notes about what your child knows, and when, will prove invaluable as their journey advances. This kind of assessment is the basic method that literacy researchers use to see which letters kids know.

If index cards feel too clinical for you, check letter-name knowledge using whatever materials or circumstances feel fun to you and your child. You can write letters anywhere—in sand at the beach, on a plate with syrup, in shaving cream on the side of the bathtub. The important thing is to take note of your child's response to the question *What letter is this?*

DRAW ATTENTION TO LETTERS AND THEIR SHAPES. Remember that the distinctions between a letter, a number, and other writing and drawings are not immediately apparent to young children. These are things that they learn slowly and through repeated attention, experience, and explanation.

Start the process by pointing out the differences among the symbols you see in storybooks and daily life. Bring your child's attention to letters wherever you encounter them. Point to them, trace them, and have your child do the same, so you know they are locked in on these particular symbols.

Analyses of parent-child conversations have found salient differences in the *content* of parents' alphabet talk. When you encounter a letter in a book, on a sign, or elsewhere in the world, talk about it in many ways. Describe its size, color, or shape, for example. Any description could build helpful knowledge and vocabulary, but *only one* of those characteristics—the shape—speaks directly to the letter's essential visual identity and builds the early-literacy foundation we're after.

When kids first start to focus on letter shapes at around 3 years old, many letters look alike to them—both lowercase p and lowercase q are circles with lines attached, and differentiating left from right can take time. Same for lowercase b and d.

To help your child notice differences among letters, make a point of talking about the curves, lines, hooks, humps, and dots, as well as the breaks and junctures within them. Those five descriptive words provide the main vocabulary you need to consistently and helpfully describe letters for your child. For example, you can highlight things like where the curve begins and ends in a C or where the lines intersect in an X. You can compare how there is one hump in the letter n and two in m; trace the long hook in an uppercase J; point out the dots in i and j; and so on. Visit readingforourlives .com/letters to download printable resources for letter teaching.

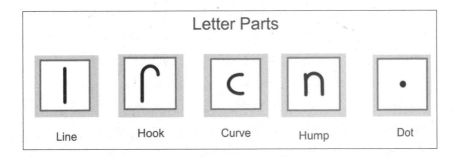

SING, THEN SAY, THE ABCS. Many parents' alphabet-teaching efforts begin and end with "The Alphabet Song." While it's fun to sing it in the car or around the house, usually there's no reference made to print while doing it, so kids aren't making the connection between the lyrics and the individual letters that make up the song. Moreover, in the song, the letters are all blurred together, leaving L-M-N-O-P sounding more like *ellaminnowpee*. Singing the song is great for building another skill—learning alphabetic order—and giving kids an introduction to letter names. But to help kids connect all the dots sooner, try sometimes saying the song, versus only singing it, and pointing to each letter as you articulate it.

ENCOURAGE MAKING LETTERS HOWEVER THEY CAN. Letter talk also spurs kids' experiments with forming the letters themselves—whether by writing them or making the shapes out of Play-Doh or Popsicle sticks. And that tactile experience with letters, in turn, creates even more opportunities for kids to ponder and engage with letters' distinctive features. A virtuous circle!

There are countless variations and activities for teaching letters. Kids can trace letters, draw them in Jell-O, make them out of macaroni, or build them from sticks. The important thing to remember (before you fall down the rabbit hole of letter activities on Pinterest) is that the lesson is in your voice and your description of the letters' form and function. If you're not talking about the letters' lines, curves, names, and sounds, your child isn't getting what they need.

TEACH UNKNOWN LETTERS FROM EASIEST TO HARDEST. Many classrooms take a letter-a-week approach and march through the alphabet from A to Z. Don't follow that example. Kids vary greatly in which letters they know when, and your instruction should reflect their individuality. Spend more time and energy on the letters your child doesn't know, and teach the unknown letters from easiest to hardest.

All kids pick up some letters more easily than others, based on factors that include the distinctiveness of their shape, their order in the alphabet, and how frequently they appear in print. Studies have found evidence that the first initial of the child's name and the letters O, B, and A are among the easiest to name and write.

Often, we parents make a big deal out of names, showing the child their name in print, teaching them to write it, or labeling and monogramming belongings with it. Many learn the name of their initial first because of the special attention parents have given that letter and its personal relevance. In fact, one study found that kids whose parents had emphasized their first initial at 3 and 4 years old tended to be stronger readers at the end of kindergarten.

Except for a kid's own first initial, O is generally the easiest letter to learn, because of its distinctive circular shape and the similarity of its uppercase and lowercase versions. Research suggests that kids tend to learn U and V last. These trends have been documented across a wide array of early-childhood programs, including Head Start, public pre-kindergarten, and private childcare settings.

There's no definitive sequence, but researchers have called the following a "typical order" for letter-name acquisition. It may be useful to refer to this order in teaching your own child—but again, responding to their interests and knowledge is most important.

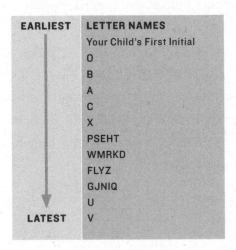

EARLIEST	LETTER NAMES
	Your Child's First Initial
	O
	B
	A
	C
	X
	PSEHT
	WMRKD
	FLYZ
	GJNIQ
	U
LATEST	V

And there's no strong evidence to support teaching only one letter a week, as many teachers do. In fact, a faster pace of letter instruction seems especially beneficial for the lowest-performing children.

Help Off the Shelf

Literacy skill work gets a bad rap. Teachers and parents decry the early onset of "drill and kill," but there are many ways to deepen understanding of letter shapes, names, sounds, and functions without resorting to long lectures or intense practice. In fact, it's best to just get in the habit of pointing out letters briefly and repeatedly through the course of everyday life. You can remind yourself to talk about letters by keeping physical prompts at hand, like alphabet books, puzzles, and wall charts.

Alphabet puzzles give kids a feel for the look and shape of letters. Go for the large, 3D letter-block variety that fits the letter shapes into predefined slots on a puzzle board, versus a flat jigsaw.

When the puzzle pieces are letter-shaped, whether uppercase or lowercase, they draw kids' attention to the lines, curves, and angles of letters, and tucking the letters into the appropriate slots requires getting the left/right and top/bottom orientation right, too. A number of vendors make personalized name puzzles, so kids can play with letters of individual significance. The pieces should be large enough that a toddler can grasp and place them with ease.

Alphabet books can prompt valuable thought and discussion about letters—if you choose them wisely, read them thoughtfully, and explain them intentionally.

The "A is for . . ." format is so familiar to parents that we can overlook its complexity. Even the most basic ABC book requires extensive background knowledge and language to understand.

Researchers estimate that kids pick up, on average, fewer than three new letters after four readings of an alphabet book. So again, the point is that we've got to stay at it over time and seize a variety of opportunities to make letter lessons stick.

To make sense of an alphabet book on their own, kids would need to know the letter names, shapes, and sounds, as well as the label given to the object shown on the page. How's a kid to know that D is for *dog* as opposed to *puppy*, *Spot*, *beagle*, or any other label that comes to mind when they see a dog picture? There's only one right answer when puzzling out the connections among a particular set of letters, words, and images in alphabet books, and grasping those shared meanings offers crucial entrée into the larger literate world, children's literature critic Perry Nodelman has observed.

"That might seem somehow limiting and repressive—and it is," Nodelman muses. "But to not be limited or repressed in this way, to not know how to solve the puzzle as intended, would be to stand outside language altogether, to be incapable of communicating or sharing the world with others . . . In teaching young readers how to solve puzzles as others expect—to share meanings—alphabet books allow them important access to the community they belong to."

In the beginning, it's not the print on the page alone, but parents' pauses, pointing, and conversation that allow kids' alphabetic knowledge to grow. Talk around an alphabet book might include things like: *This page says "A is for Apple." This is the letter A.* (Point to A.) *A makes the /a/ sound. Can you say /a/? Can you hear that* apple *starts with /a/? A-P-P-L-E spells* apple. (Point to each letter.)

Environmental print—the signs, product labels, and logos that we encounter in everyday life—also makes impactful teaching tools. Even better, such print is readily available for incidental teaching, infinitely useful, and generally free. Many parents point to words and read them aloud at home, during play, and while out and about in their communities, without any prompting. But far fewer bring their children's attention to the level of individual letters embedded in the signs and labels.

Researchers found evidence that a program that coached middle-socioeconomic-status parents in how to focus their 2- to 5-year-olds' attention on specific letters using multisensory strategies led to significant improvement in letter knowledge and environmental-print reading ability. The strategies encompassed pointing (visual), saying (auditory), moving (kinesthetic), and tracing (tactile). Importantly, the program taught parents to use directional language (the terms *up*, *down*, *around*, and *across*) to describe how the letters are formed, which helps kids notice and recall their distinctive features.

All parents should have environmental print strategies in their toolkits, but it's especially useful for those who lack access to a wide variety of quality books at home (or the time to read extensively at home). The signs around your neighborhood and the labels on your clothes and home products have everything you need to support your young child's emergent literacy. If you're folding laundry, for example, pull out a graphic tee or a shirt with a logo, trace a letter, talk about it and ask your child to do the same. I counted twenty-two different letters on a Trader Joe's paper grocery bag alone. Between the store name, website address, instructions to hold both handles, call to reuse and recycle, and illustration of Cidre Mousseux, we had the alphabet minus K, Q, V, and Z. That's fodder for many rounds of letter I Spy.

Ibi Zoboi, a Haitian American author of young adult fiction, spoke powerfully about this during a panel at the Texas Book Festival. Zoboi said she grew up in an environment where there were "absolutely no bookstores around," but she was not without rich stories and language exposure. She said that her love of speculative fiction grew from the political tales often embellished with magical realism that her mom, aunt, and other relatives told about their home country. And she gleaned volumes from their words and the everyday language around her home.

"I'm a child of the '80s and I watched a lot of TV," she explains. "When people asked me what were the books that I loved growing up, I cannot always say, but I don't want anybody to look down on me or any children like myself who did not have books in the home. We had TV and that's also a form of storytelling. We had the back of cereal boxes. Magazines."

Work with what you've got to give your kids the lessons that they need most. Unlike classroom teachers who have limited time, myriad goals, and kids of varying abilities and prior knowledge, parents have a limited number of children and years of everyday interactions. For the most part, your success will boil down to time and consistency. Don't worry about making mistakes. There's no perfect instruction. Just get talking, so your child can get learning.

Try This at Home
Give Letters Shape

The importance of diving into letter names, sounds, and shapes when kids are as young as 3 cannot be overstated. Preschoolers are fully capable of learning these building blocks of reading. And parents can make it fun and gradual by introducing letters lightly over time in everyday life through books, signage, labels, monograms, toys, and other print.

Easy does it, and emphasizing the letter shapes is the way to go for parents. Any time you spend describing letters' curves and lines brings your child's attention to defining features, helps them distinguish among letters, and supports writing. Plus, this talk also often naturally segues into discussing letter names and sounds. For example, if you were teaching a child to spell their name you might say things like the following.

Z-O-R-A spells *Zora.*

This is a Z. Z says /z/. It's made of two short lines and one long line. It goes this way to the right and back down this way to the left and then over this way to the right. (Write the letter.) Can you say /z/? Can you write a Z?

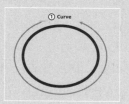

This is O. It is a big circle. You write it by starting here and making a curve all the way around. (Write the letter.) Can you say /ō/? Can you write an O?

This is the letter R. It's made of one long line. (Trace the line.) One curve. (Trace the curve.) And one short line. (Trace the short line.) Trace the R with your finger like this. (Demonstrate.) R says /r/. Can you say /r/?

Look at this letter A. It's made of two long lines and one short line. Can you make the letter A? A says /a/. Can you say /a/?

————JOURNAL PROMPTS————

- What does your child know about letters? Can they tell a letter apart from drawings or numbers?

- Which uppercase and lowercase letters can your child name if they see them?

- What print do you have in your home and neighborhood that you can call attention to (e.g., magnetic letters, monogrammed items, books, and magazines)? Where could you add more print to your home, such as framed letter art or favorite quotes?

- When writing on their own, does your child use letters at all? If so, which letters do they write? Does their writing reflect the knowledge that letters represent sounds?

9

Word Wisdom: How to Spell Your Way to Better Reading

For, though the origin of most of our words is forgotten, each word was at first a stroke of genius, and obtained currency, because for the moment it symbolized the world to the first speaker and to the hearer. The etymologist finds the deadest word to have been once a brilliant picture.

—Ralph Waldo Emerson

I hail from Akron, Ohio, a city most famous (depending on who you ask) for being the former rubber capital of the world, the birthplace of LeBron James, or the site of Sojourner Truth's "Ain't I a Woman" speech in 1851. But not until Zaila Avant-garde, a black girl from Harvey, Louisiana, won the Scripps National Spelling Bee in 2021 did I hear of another of my hometown's claims to fame: Akronite MacNolia Cox was the first black student to make it to the final round of the National Spelling Bee—in 1936.

Today the Scripps National Spelling Bee is among the most diverse academic competitions around, but in Cox's day, vicious segregation marred her ascent to the national stage. Poet A. Van Jordan, another Akron native, excavated Cox's incredible story by obtaining information at the city's Department of Vital Statistics and snippets from Cox's mother's diary, which had been preserved by a family member. Cox had to ride in segregated train cars, take back stairs, enter banquets through the kitchen, and stay at the home of a black surgeon in D.C. because the Willard Hotel, where the other spellers stayed, wouldn't welcome her.

Cox spelled flawlessly in round after round of the national competition. Meanwhile her white competitors misspelled words and were allowed to remain in the competition due to technicalities. When she looked destined to win, spelling bee officials gave her a word that wasn't on the approved list: *Nemesis*, the name of the Greek goddess of divine retribution and revenge, a proper noun and, by the competition's own laws at the time, verboten. She spelled it incorrectly and was knocked out of the competition. She went home to Ohio, where scholarships she'd been promised never materialized, and she died of cancer, a domestic, at age 53.

Jordan's poetic retelling of her story, *M-A-C-N-O-L-I-A*, published in 2006, tells Cox's life story in reverse from her deathbed to the night before the historic spelling bee, the moment of her highest potential. In an article "The Word Is 'Nemesis': The Fight to Integrate the National Spelling Bee," historian Cynthia Greenlee captures the larger significance of the story: "Historically, African-Americans have understood the spelling bee as a contested racial space, where mastering a word list was a feat of skill, motivation, and racial resistance through direct competition with one's 'social betters,'" she writes. "If black spellers weren't actually sparring with white rivals, each word memorized—the letters, language of origin, possible meanings—was another symbolic brick building a black community hungry for the book-learning denied to them in slavery and segregation."

Much of the media coverage of Avant-garde's victory noted contemporary injustices that result in few black competitive spellers—expensive travel costs and competition fees, lack of sponsorships, and the fact that schools with many black children have fewer resources to support and train students. And it's true that coaches like the fictional English professor Dr. Larabee in the movie *Akeelah and the Bee* are scarce and pricey. Many former Scripps Bee winners and finalists charge more than $100 an hour to groom the next generation of competitors.

But the inequity is deeper and longer-standing than mere access to a spelling bee. And Avant-garde, a homeschooled phenom and three-time Guinness World Record holder for basketball dribbling, is the kind of exception that accentuates the rule. She had to be extraordinary in so many ways to win her national title. The average child in America today—black or white—needs access to spelling instruction itself, let alone in-depth study of letter patterns, language nuances, and word meanings.

Four Things Parents Need to Know about Spelling

As adults, we know that the professional world judges spelling mistakes severely. Errors in job applications and résumés tend to bias recruiters against candidates and harm career advancement, studies show. What we may not fully appreciate is that the consequences of spelling woes emerge in elementary school, long before students enter the workforce.

Here are four things you need to know now about how spelling impacts your child—and how you can impact their spelling:

Spelling is integral to developing into a reader and writer.
Spelling is the glue that sticks words in memory, renders
them instantly recognizable in print, and makes reading them
quicker and more fluent. Research studies suggest that the
more accurate and stable your memory of a word's spelling,
the faster you'll read the word. Spelling knowledge has
been directly linked to sight-word reading, reading fluency,
and even third-grade reading achievement scores. And
evidence suggests that explicit spelling instruction improves
students' spelling, as you would expect, while also
supporting better phonological awareness and reading
skills.

**Spelling errors negatively bias teacher assessments in
schools, even when that's not the focus of their grading.**
Appearances matter so much that it's hard for teachers to
separate the content of student writing (the knowledge it
displays, arguments it makes, and quality of supporting
evidence) from its presentation (handwriting, spelling, and
grammar). Teachers struggle to fairly and validly view the
substance of work that has spelling issues. Thus, students
who struggle with spelling are at risk of receiving lower
grades in other subjects and having their competency
overlooked.

Spelling is generally neglected in schools. Researchers have
described spelling instruction as "the abandoned stepchild
in the family of language arts." Many teachers devote
minimal minutes to it per day, even though many students

experience substantial spelling difficulty, by teachers' own reports. Others spend considerable time on spelling instruction but rely on practices that they know don't work. In numerous surveys, the vast majority of elementary school teachers say spelling is inadequately addressed in the curriculum.

Parents can make a huge difference. As with so many other areas of literacy development, parents are particularly well positioned to spur this high-impact skill. You can facilitate regular exposure to print that helps kids pick up on patterns on their own and you can teach spelling directly. And remember, even if you're not a spelling champ, your skills are surely better than your preschooler's.

Through the years, you'll observe volumes of authentic writing in the lists, letters, and stories kids pen at home. They are great fodder to identify the words your child wants to use, those they struggle with, and what you should teach next. (If you're ready to assess their spelling chops and they haven't written anything at home lately, suggest they draw up a birthday or present wish list or write to a relative.)

Free from the confines of rigid school schedules, you have more time than teachers to instruct your child on the spellings of individual words, when and how they're needed. You're also a ready resource to respond to in-the-moment spelling questions and challenges that pop up. This doesn't mean hours of drills or forgoing more relaxed playtime: a little spelling instruction, offered consistently, goes a long way.

How Parents Can Spur Spelling

Successful storytime means a comfy setting, good books, and page-turning performances. By comparison, spelling with your child feels stripped down, a cappella rather than musical theater. There's no deferring to an author's words, an illustrator's images, or a character's voice to guide the lessons or drive engagement. Still, talking about words and segmenting them into letters can bring a mindfulness, care, and engagement to family life that's just as vital and powerful as a read-aloud.

Parents have ample occasion, through the days and years, to meaningfully explore and cultivate spelling with our children. We've got the time—even if it doesn't always feel that way—and can build the expertise to teach kids fruitful strategies, encourage interest in words, and help them become more reflective and analytical about their writing. Here are eight ways to support strong spelling at home.

CONSISTENTLY DRAW ATTENTION TO PRINT. Kids learn a lot about spelling without being explicitly taught, and this learning begins as soon as they pay attention to written words, typically around 3 years old. Their environments—the books, signs, and other text around—provide the raw material for subconscious learning. Whenever kids lock in on the letters in books, on signs, on toys, and elsewhere, they soak up and analyze visual characteristics of written language.

Kids instinctively pick up the relative frequency of different letter combinations from repeated exposure to writing in their environment, and they apply this statistical knowledge to even their earliest spelling attempts. This unconscious awareness of visual patterns in spelling develops long before they learn that letters represent speech sounds or start trying to spell phonetically. For example, preschoolers tend to write common letters (E, T, and A) more often than infrequent ones (e.g., J, Q, and Z) in those seemingly random strings of letters they produce early on. Letters from their own names, and letter combinations in alphabetic order, are over-represented in their scribblings. Their writing attempts reflect the print they've noticed most and what the people in their lives have taught them.

Researchers call this process "statistical learning," because these spelling efforts are informed by how frequently a child has seen let-ters appear in certain combinations, orders, and positions. Chil-dren aren't consciously counting the instances of certain sequences or calculating probabilities, but they've gathered the data and syn-thesized it to inform their own writing, nonetheless. And the more complex, contextual, or rare the pattern, the harder it is and longer it takes to grasp subconsciously. Patterns that exist in one circum-stance but not another are especially tricky. (Think of spelling the short /o/ sound with an A after W or QU—like in *swab, squad,* or *wallet*—but spelling it with O otherwise—like in *odd, body,* or *olive.*)

Parents aid statistical learning by facilitating lots of exposure to print. In the beginning, this requires an adult directing the child—for instance, pointing to the text accompanying an illustration in a picture book, or their name on a piece of paper.

ENCOURAGE WRITING. Although spelling bee contestants spell aloud to demonstrate their mastery, your child's earliest attempts will likely be on paper. Nurture their writing by always having paper and crayons or colored pencils on hand for them to scribble away long before they can write letters we'd recognize. It's a joy to behold the creations that a stack of index cards and a pencil in the back seat of the car can inspire.

Children as young as 2 or 3 years old demonstrate some knowledge of writing, even if they have no idea yet that it connects with spoken language. Pretend-writing grocery lists, restaurant menus, signs, and so on as a part of play at home is a precursor to spelling, too. One day you may notice that those scribbles are running from left to right and top to bottom on the page. Another day some conventional-looking letters may start popping up amid the slashes and squiggles.

You can ask them what their writing says and even transcribe a traditional version of it below their scribbles. *Way to write! What does this say? I see. I would write that this way: The dog is happy.* (Point to each word as you say it.) Bonus: you get a record of funny stories to revisit and share as they grow.

APPLAUD EARLY SPELLING. The early quality of your child's spelling reflects things we've been talking about throughout this book: their phonemic awareness, letter knowledge, and the associations they make between the two. With reading, the letters are given to them and they have to sift through their knowledge of a limited set of sounds to approximate a pronunciation. With spelling, they're hearing a word, segmenting the sounds, and settling on one letter sequence from numerous possible combinations.

A child's first attempts at spelling specific words you offer may be wild. They might spell *kite* A-G-H. And that's okay. Don't even bother correcting it. Remember that we explored in Chapter 3 the value of praising the process. Say *I see you are working hard on your letters and writing* and move on. The child clearly hasn't mastered letter-sound matching lessons, so it's alphabetic principle work, not spelling lessons, that they need at that point. When their spellings of *kite* start to look more phonetic, like K-T, you'll know they've progressed, and your approach can evolve, too. Then you can say something like *You listened well to the sounds in* kite. *You've written the letters that say the sounds at the beginning and end of* kite. *Do you hear the middle sound in* kite, *too? I hear an /ī/.* Kite *is spelled K-I-T-E.* (Write each letter as you say it.)

Giving kids the freedom to invent their own spellings doesn't interfere with their ability to learn conventional spellings later. In fact, researchers say the exact opposite is true: "Allowing children to engage in the analytical process of invented spelling, followed by appropriate feedback, has been found to facilitate learning to read and spell, not hamper the process."

LOOK FOR THE KNOWLEDGE THEY DEMONSTRATE. Parents' assessments of kids' spelling usually amounts to deeming an attempt right or wrong. But that black-and-white thinking doesn't serve kids. To teach, we have to learn to see shades of gray. In this context, that means looking at misspellings with an eye for what kids know about sounds, letters, and the relationships between them. For example, ask yourself what's "right" within a misspelling. Does the writing show conventional letters? Is the initial sound of the word represented (e.g., spelling *cat* with K-T)? Are all the sounds represented? Are some letters in the proper sequence? This kind of analysis of kids' spelling is your window into their knowledge base.

And while it's convenient to envision learners progressing through set phases—say, from spelling phonetically to applying spelling patterns to taking word meaning and word origin into consideration—they don't. The process is much messier. You'll need to make your assessments word by word because kids show some knowledge of letter sequences before they learn how letters and sounds connect. They spell some words flawlessly from the start because of the experiences they've had and attention they've paid to them. All kinds of factors play a role in their learning, from the complexity of the word to the number of exposures they've had to it and what lessons they've received in relevant letter sequences and spelling patterns.

Understand that the journey isn't linear, try to grasp where your child is with the particular words they are trying to spell, and you'll get a better sense of how you can help. Praise and support every step on the path, and the rest will come.

Here's an example to illustrate what different spellings of a word might reveal about a child's knowledge and what a parent might say or do to affirm it. We'll get into more specifics about what kids are expected to know by kindergarten and after toward the end of this chapter.

DESCRIPTION	EXAMPLE	SAMPLE RESPONSE
Scribbles. Writing but without conventional letters. No grasp of the connections between letters and sounds.	*BABIES* AS 	*Great job working on your writing.*
Seemingly random letters. Shows some awareness of letters versus numbers and other written symbols, but doesn't yet connect them to sounds. May reflect statistical knowledge about the likelihood of certain letter combinations, but not the sounds in the word.	*BABIES* AS ARG	*I see the letters A, R, and G. You are working hard on your writing.*
Initial sound represented. Makes a clear connection between the initial sound in the word and the letter that represents it.	*BABIES* AS B	*Yes,* babies *starts with the letter B. B says /b/.*

DESCRIPTION	EXAMPLE	SAMPLE RESPONSE
One or more letters in proper sequence. Showing awareness of letter-sound connections beyond the first letter.	*BABIES* AS BA	Yes, babies *starts with the letters B and A. I see you wrote a B and an A. Way to put the letters in order!*
All phonemes represented, but some vowels or consonants may be off. Demonstrates strong phonemic awareness and uses a letter to indicate each sound within the word.	*BABIES* AS BABEZ	*You have written all the sounds in* babies. Babies *does start with B-A-B!*
Conventional representation. Has full command of the alphabetic principle and has strong familiarity with common nonphonetic spelling patterns and conventions.	*BABIES* AS BABIES	*Great job paying attention to all the letters in the word!*

RESPOND TO THEIR QUESTIONS AND INTERESTS. Answering your child's questions about words, and responding to words they want to write, should be central to your instruction. Kids learn to spell, in part, through continuous attention to the print they encounter (and produce) in regular life. As you go about your day, be alert to words that exemplify concepts and patterns that are ripe for review or introduction. These could be in recipes, street signs, pleasure reading, or eventually in homework.

When my daughter was younger, I read the stories, notes, and lists she wrote at school and at home and (subtly) kept a running list on my phone of the words she misspelled. I then made a point to spend some time casually teaching them. Depending on the word, I might tell a story about its origin, relate it to a word she spelled correctly, or give a quick lesson in the patterns it embodied.

TALK ABOUT MEANINGFUL UNITS OF WORDS. Some spelling programs treat the meaning-carrying units within words like suffixes and prefixes as advanced word content for kids to tackle later in elementary school or even middle school. The truth is, though, that many of these elements are well within the grasp of younger children. You could say to a kindergartener: *When you put* un *in front of some words, it means the opposite of the base word.* Unsafe *means not safe.* Unsure *means not sure.* From there, they can apply the idea in all kinds of ways and tell you about the unhappy kid on the playground or a character who celebrated an "unbirthday" in a story they read.

TEACH HELPFUL PATTERNS. The sound awareness and letter knowledge we explored in previous chapters give kids the experience and insights they need to apply the alphabetic principle and spell straightforward words easily. But there are twenty-six letters and forty-four speech sounds in English. There are also 250 or more ways to spell those sounds. Silent letters, single letters representing multiple sounds, and a slew of sounds with the same pronunciation but different spellings all make English special.

When there are multiple plausible options, spellers need more than letter-sound knowledge to choose the correct one. To instill spellings such as when the /f/ sound is represented by PH or when G goes silent in *sign* and *night*, we have to venture into a discussion of spelling patterns, word meanings, and word origins.

Researchers have identified a few helpful categories of patterns to consider. These include letters whose pronunciation may change depending on the surrounding letters or sounds, how some sequences are more common in certain positions within words, and cases where meaning factors in. If you know a pattern, teach it. And when you don't, look it up and teach it later. More on that in the next section.

LEARN AS YOU GO. If you're thinking you don't have the knowledge necessary to teach your child spelling patterns, you're not alone. There are lots of ways to gain it, and they don't require reading a textbook from cover to cover or enrolling in grad school. Pick up a copy of an accessible reference book like *The Complete Guide to English Spelling Rules* to dip into whenever you want to clarify something—like when C makes a soft sound like in *cent, cinch*, or *cycle* (when it precedes E, I, and Y) and when it's hard like in *car, come*, and *curtain* (when it precedes A, O, and U).

You can also take small actions to slowly accumulate language tidbits you can draw on when your child asks how something is spelled—or why. For example, you might follow Merriam-Webster Dictionary and Scripps Spelling Bee on Instagram, sign up for a word-origin newsletter, or subscribe to a linguist's podcast. Most parents don't have time to do a deep dive into word histories (nor is it necessary), so it's best to find ways to add a steady trickle of insights into the media diet you already consume. Visit readingforourlives.com/spelling for my latest resource recommendations.

Can You Spell C-O-N-V-E-R-S-A-T-I-O-N?

Young kids love a good tale and can appreciate the stories behind how words come into existence. That history brings spelling to life, makes teaching time more fun, and helps answer the perpetual question of why many words aren't spelled the way they sound. Plus, stories make spellings stick in our memories better than just staring at or copying words. Here's a quick list of typical ways words get their spellings. Use it to jump-start your and your child's curiosity and discussion around individual words and their components.

1. **Absorption.** English swallows words from other languages whole, spelling included, especially where food is concerned. *Quiche, pizza, tortilla*, anyone? Over time and with instruction, kids can recognize that words derived from certain places tend to spell sounds a certain way—such as French-derived words using CH for /sh/, as in *chalet, chauffeur,* and *chivalry.*

    When dining out or visiting specialty food markets, point out spelling trends you observe. *Look at all the double Ts on this menu:* biscotti, spaghetti, bruschetta, ciabatta*!* (Point.) *I know some other Italian words with double Ts that are common in English:* terra-cotta, motto, stiletto, confetti. When playing restaurant at home, order up something tasty and deliver a side of spelling by sharing how the item is spelled and why.

2. **Compounding.** Putting two independent words together to form a new one is a nearly universal method of creating more complex words, across languages. But the meanings of some pairings are more transparent than others. Think *doorbell* versus *hogwash.* When kids recognize that a rattlesnake is a snake that rattles, they have a better shot at spelling it right than if they approached it letter by letter.

    These examples are easy to point out to kids during routine activities. Parents might say: *Sometimes we put two words together to make a new word. For example,* after *and* noon *make* afternoon. Bed *and* room *make* bedroom. Birth *and* day *make* birthday. *When you're spelling words like these, think of the smaller words inside and spell those.*

3. **Imitation.** The spellings of some words, *onomatopoeias*, are influenced by the sound of the item or action they refer to. Think of comic book favorites like *boom, pow,* and *splat* or *hiss, ping,* and *whack.* Some, like *cuckoo,* have been present with various spellings since Middle English.

   This is a playful type of word to introduce to young children. Tell them, for example: Onomatopoeia *is such a fun word. This kind of word gets its name by imitating a natural sound. For example, the word* buzz *sounds like a bee's buzz and the word* hiss *sounds like a snake's hiss. When we sing "Old McDonald Had a Farm," all those sounds—the cow's moo, the chick's cluck, and the pig's oink—are onomatopoeias!*

4. **Naming.** English takes names and turns them into words, too. Called *eponyms,* these name-inspired words include *leotard, hypnosis,* and *Mary Janes. Proprietary eponyms* include words like *Kleenex, Post-it, Crockpot,* and *Breathalyzer.* They were born of brands that got so popular that their names came to stand in for the whole product class.

   Creating words from names is particularly prevalent in medicine, where diseases, symptoms, and tests are often christened after their supposed discoverers, such as Alzheimer's disease, Hodgkin's lymphoma, and Crohn's disease. (Fun fact: some physicians think it's time to abandon eponyms because they don't describe conditions as well as more scientific names and they don't reflect the group effort involved in medical discovery.)

   When you encounter such words, point them out to your child: *The dress code says that you have to wear Mary Janes with your uniform. Mary Janes are dress shoes with a strap across the top. They got their name from a character in the* Buster Brown *comic strip that launched in the* New York Herald *in 1902.*

5. **Abbreviation.** Collections of initials, or "acronyms," can be pronounced either letter by letter, like *CNN* (Cable News Network), or as single words, like *NASA* (National Aeronautics and Space Administration) or *GOAT* (greatest of all time). Words can also be shortened by dropping off the end, such as *adorbs* for *adorable* and *rando* for *random.*

   Again, these are types of words and terms you'll come across often with your kids. Don't assume they know what they mean. Instead, explain, for example, *The* USA *in* Team USA *stands for United States of America. You spell USA just like it sounds— U-S-A. Just be sure to capitalize each letter.*

6. **Blending.** Combining parts of two words to create a new one has given us *frenemy* (friend + enemy), *glamping* (glamour + camping), and *cosplay* (costume + play). In *Through the Looking Glass,* author Lewis Carroll named the blends that he created— like *mimsy* (miserable + flimsy) and *slithy* (lithe + slimy)— *portmanteaus,* after stiff leather suitcases opening into two compartments.

   Blends show up regularly when *Merriam-Webster* releases lists of new words and definitions it's adding to its dictionary. You could tell your child: Faux-hawk *was just added to the dictionary. It's a combination of* faux, *which means fake, and* Mohawk, *which is a haircut where the sides are shaved and the remaining hair is upright down the middle of the scalp. With a faux-hawk, the hair could be gathered or slicked up to the middle instead of being completely shaved off.* Faux *is spelled F-A-U-X.*

7. **Repurposing.** Taking an existing word and giving it a new meaning is yet another way to make a new word. Technologies are frequent culprits. *Tablet, catfish, block,* even *copy* and *paste* all have taken on fresh meanings in the internet era while maintaining the familiar spellings.

   You can tell your child, *The word* cloud *is spelled C-L-O-U-D whether you're talking about the water vapor floating high in the sky or the place where your Google Classroom assignments are stored. When people created software that could be delivered through the internet, they used the image of a cloud to represent the big network they hoped to create. The name stuck.*

   Use backstories and explanations like these to keep conversations about words and language going in your home. The attention you foster to individual words and the letters within them will help your child deploy their statistical learning skills better and they will benefit more from the direct instruction, too.

Pace Yourself

Unlike many subject areas we've covered, there is not yet consensus on the best order of spelling instruction. While working one-on-one with your child, look to state guidelines for ideas about what to teach when, though *not* for how fast to move along. With a typically developing child, unhindered by the time and attention constraints of a classroom setting, you'll likely be able to move at a faster clip than a teacher can in an academic year. Additionally, you'll be able to introduce layers of word origin, history, meaning, and structure from the start.

Here's a partial list of the knowledge and skills kids should attain grade by grade, culled from the Common Core State Standards, Texas state standards, and expert recommendations. Again, keep in mind that the following grade-level designations should be thought of as minimum criteria. Go as fast as your child's interest and knowledge retention allow.

KINDERGARTEN

- Spot, name, and form letters.
- Understand that letters can represent speech sounds in writing.
- Write a letter or letters for most consonant and short-vowel sounds.
- Segment and count the speech sounds within words.
- Spell words with regular consonant and vowel sounds, including these common patterns: vowel-consonant, or VC (*at*); consonant-vowel-consonant, or CVC (*sit*); and consonant-consonant-vowel-consonant, or CCVC (*flag*).
- Be able to write some high-frequency phonetically irregular words, such as *of, the, have.*

FIRST GRADE

- Distinguish and spell words with closed syllables (*mat*) and open syllables (*me*).
- Recognize and use common long-vowel patterns, such as vowel-consonant-*e,* or VCe (*name, hope, kite*), and combinations of vowels, aka "vowel teams" (*read, seed*).
- Recognize and use vowel-R syllable patterns (*burn, car, shirt*).
- Grasp the "floss rule" that the letters F, L, S, and Z are often doubled after a short vowel at the end of a word (e.g., *glass, kiss, staff, call, buzz*; exceptions: *bus, yes, this, us*).

- Spell high-frequency irregular words from a research-based list, such as the Fry or Dolch lists often used in elementary schools.
- Use suffixes that mark tense, plurals, and the third person (e.g., *-s*, *-es*, *-ed*, *-ing*, *-er*, and *-est*).
- Use prefixes and suffixes that don't change base-word pronunciation or spelling (e.g., *un-*, *re-*, *dis-*, *-ful*).
- Spell compound words with common base words and consistent pronunciation (e.g., *football, Sunday*).
- Spell untaught words phonetically, drawing on phonemic awareness and spelling conventions.

Check out your own state standards to confirm, adjust, or add to this list. Then look for opportunities to spend a few minutes nurturing the skills most relevant to your child. For example, with a beginner, you can snag a piece of paper and write a VC, CVC, or CCVC word (e.g., *at, bat,* or *chat*) on it, then tell your child what you know about it. You might say: *When C and H are together they can say /ch/, like in* cheese *and* chair. *Can you say /ch/? What happens when you put /ch/ and /at/ together? Yes,* chat. *How would you spell* chat? *Yes, C-H-A-T.*

A Few Lessons from Bee Parents

Beyond the importance of spelling for reading, I love it as a subject for parents to teach because there's great documentation of parents taking young children from spelling novices to masters. The parents of kids like 2021 Scripps national champion Zaila Avant-garde offer an interesting (if extreme) case study in literacy-focused parenting. The so-called bee parents that anthropologist and author Shalini Shankar documented in *Beeline: What Spelling Bees Reveal about*

Generation Z's New Path to Success place enormous value on education and devote considerable time to supporting their children's learning. So even if our aim isn't to pit our kids against the 476,000 words in *Webster's Third New International Dictionary Unabridged*, there are a few essential lessons we can draw from their approach.

ACT ON YOUR PRIORITIES. Many parents say they value academics, but an honest look at how they spend their time and money may reveal otherwise. Bee parents invest consistently and wholeheartedly in their children's spelling pursuits over many years. Edith Fuller was just 5 years old when she earned a spot in the Scripps National Spelling Bee, helped by her mom quizzing her on words in 20-minute-long sessions throughout the day.

Parents featured in *Beeline* spent hours preparing word lists and study materials for their kids. They spent money on dictionaries, word lists, coaching, and travel. Their schedules and budgets demonstrate their commitment.

Again, my point is not that we need to do exactly what they did, but rather that we can often do more to bring our own actions in line with our intentions for our children.

LEARN ALONGSIDE YOUR CHILD. *Beeline* depicts kids' development from beginner to expert spellers. But parents' growth is on display, too. The book shows parents building the research, teaching, and coaching skills they need to support their children's development. Bee parents are willing to learn, make mistakes, and grow with their kids. They model focus, dedication, and consistency over long periods.

For example, pronunciation is a perennial challenge among bee parents, whether because English is not their first language or the words are rare and seldom spoken. Numerous elite spellers that Shankar interviewed described misspelling words that they knew, because they didn't recognize the official pronunciation when it was read aloud at the competition. Their parents had pronounced the words differently during practice (e.g., pronouncing *righteous* as ri-tee-us). The kids didn't blame their parents for their errors, but together devised strategies to get better. Parents put in time to learn how to read pronunciation marks and produce the right accents, tones, and stresses.

GET OUT OF THE WAY. Bee parents can't learn the words for their kids. The spellers have to own the work, putting in hours and hours of study alone. Elite spellers routinely put in two to four hours of spelling study a day during the week and up to eight hours on holidays and weekends. Avant-garde says she studied seven hours a day to prep for her championship run. As they age from elementary to middle schoolers, they take increasing ownership of the process, devising their own study methods, practice routines, and even software to meet their needs. Ideally, bee parents support without coddling, and their kids learn to persevere with poise and positivity.

Indeed, Shankar, *Beeline*'s author, witnessed Zaila Avant-garde's third-round elimination in the 2019 National Spelling Bee on the word *vagaries*. Two years later, Avant-garde won the cup by correctly spelling *murraya*, a genus of tropical Asiatic and Australian trees. Shankar attributes the elite speller's "astounding progress" to "tremendous work ethic, extraordinary aptitude, and a whole lot of parental investment and support."

Avant-garde credits her dad with noticing and nurturing her spelling gifts. She invested in herself, too, reportedly spending her $10,000 prize winnings from a 2020 online spelling bee to pay for study materials and private tutoring from a past Scripps Bee runner-up. It just goes to show that when we support kids' academic interests, they learn how to get themselves to their own next level.

Try This at Home
Focus on the Fun

When tackling a list of spelling words (whether sent from school or ones that you've noticed your child misspells), you should encourage your child to *analyze* the word, as well as their own attempts to spell it, not simply to stare at the words or copy them repeatedly. Analysis helps kids learn words inside and out and bolsters reading skill.

A good starting place is with a research-backed spelling practice that's known (descriptively) as the "look-say-cover-write-check" routine. For example, let's imagine you're teaching the word *build* because your child leaves out the U. With this method, you would write the word with the unusual or commonly mistaken part in bold or underlined. Then tell your child that the marked part is the *fun* part—the opportunity to get curious about letter sequences, sound patterns, word meaning, origins, and more. Don't call it the hard part if your aim is to boost engagement rather than heighten anxiety.

Then you'd have your child follow these six simple steps:

1. **Look** at the correctly spelled word with the unusual part in bold or underlined.

2. **Say** the word. *Build.*

3. **Cover** the word or close their eyes, and try to visualize the word in their mind.

4. **Write** the word on paper. Just once!

5. **Check** for correctness by comparing the written word to the model.

6. If incorrect, get curious about the nature of the error and copy the word correctly.

It's worth your time to help your child engage with (and hopefully "memorize") challenging words by focusing on their sound, meaning, and construction; practicing recalling the spelling; comparing their spelling to the model; and fixing mistakes. The self-evaluation and self-correction steps in the practice routine pack the power.

Through it all, remember that your main aim is to teach how the English spelling system works. You want to show kids how to analyze and think about the regularities and irregularities in the words they encounter—on lists and in the wild—not force them to stare at words and hope to magically absorb them.

JOURNAL PROMPTS

- What did you learn about spelling that you want to act on with your child?

- What strategies will you use to encourage your child to write every day, from lists and letters to stories and poems?

- Where will you make a note of words that your child is struggling to spell?

- How will you provide opportunities to analyze the correct spellings?

10

Extra Credit: How Savvy Parents Keep Learning

Knowledge is of two kinds. We know a subject ourselves, or we know where we can find information upon it.

—Samuel Johnson

Every parent has their own idiosyncratic cabinet of advisors they rely upon, often our pediatricians, relatives, and friends. This suggests that convenience is a major factor in who we're listening to—the people we are closest to, plus the medical professionals we see at regular intervals—for help on our parenting journeys.

But there's no guarantee that our particular sources (however well intentioned) can provide effective advice. That realization may be a part of why you've sought out books like this one. You're right to be proactive in seeking evidence-based research and resources, because the sound bites and headlines we see in the media and often hear repeated as common knowledge tend to gloss over crucial nuance and lead us to wrong conclusions.

In the age of information overload, many parents don't want to hear that the key to better parenting for early literacy is more detail, not less. But now you know it's true. A little meaningful, intentional engagement with research, data, and science—beyond personal observation and logic—goes a long way toward boosting effectiveness, confidence, and (dare I say) enjoyment.

Keep in mind that no single study is gospel, however. That's why the recommendations in this book have been based on scientific consensus that's emerged from high-quality peer-reviewed work, including original research studies, systematic reviews, and large-scale meta-analyses.

Science is always advancing, and local education policies and curricula will shift in kind, so you'll need to continually engage with the latest information to best support your child. The way forward is to see new findings not as providing "the answer" but as an opportunity to refine our understanding—and prompt new questions. That is, research gives us chances to think, to learn, and to grow. As health writer Kim Tingley advises, think of a study's value as a slight adjustment of an eyeglass-lens prescription. "Each one answers the question 'Is it clearer like this, or like this?'" she wrote, "and in doing so, brings our view of reality—our understanding of ourselves and the world around us—into sharper focus."

———

In this book, I've cited researchers who have devoted decades of study to topics so narrow that they might show up as a single bullet point on a tip sheet or magazine article. They toiled for years to get to a level where they could conceive of a study that would add real value to the field, then they spent years testing a hypothesis to make sure the findings held up, then they hoped someone from another lab or institution would take up the topic and replicate, refine, or otherwise engage with the results. Only after all that might they take the step of trying to win wide publicity for the idea.

All that's to say that even the best research isn't immediately translatable into practical prescriptions. The time between when a finding is generally accepted among the scientific community and when related practices are widely implemented by teachers (let alone parents) is notoriously long. And it's not just in education. In the health field, the research-to-practice time lag's been pegged at an average of seventeen years. So distinct are the interests and so scant the communication among researchers and practitioners in business management that Denise Rousseau, a professor of organizational behavior and public policy at Carnegie Mellon University, thinks the term *gap* is being too generous. *Chasm* or *fault line* would be more accurate descriptors in her estimate. "Practitioners want their questions answered (now)," she observed. "The best evidence does not necessarily provide answers, and academics prefer to ask their own questions (in their own time)."

Scholars may have a reputation for toiling away in the ivory tower on obscure research to pave their way to tenure. But I've found that reading researchers (who are often parents as well) make an effort to get their best advice to the people who need it most. It's just that they want to be confident in their results before taking them to the streets—a fine and worthy impulse.

Lisa Scott, a psychology professor and the director of the Brain Cognition and Development Lab at the University of Florida, says it's important for parents to realize that study results must be replicated before researchers can be sure they're valid, not a fluke or the product of some unknown factor or mistake. Before she and her team recommended that parents make sure to read books with named characters to infants, for example, they did four studies with different methods that provided evidence that learning individual labels improves infants' cognitive abilities. "It took me a long time to really be comfortable with being able to give that advice to parents," she told me.

The tweaking and critiquing of methods and analysis in community with other researchers is the point. That's how science and knowledge advance. Then, once Scott was ready, she hustled to get the word out to parents. She published a piece in *The Conversation*, a nonprofit independent news outlet devoted to sharing expert views for the public good. She even worked with a filmmaker to put together a mini-sitcom public service announcement about reading books to babies. Her comments have been picked up in media as far-flung as the *Washington Post* and the *New Zealand Herald*. Heck, she's even tweeted about the importance of reading the right books at the right time to benefit babies' brains.

There are a few lessons for parents in this example.

IT'S WORTH YOUR WHILE TO FOLLOW NEW DEVELOPMENTS. Fresh findings and best practices for raising strong, thriving readers, writers, thinkers, and communicators will continue to emerge as research and technology advance. Plus, you may wish to pursue some of the areas touched on in this book in more depth, or dig into an area that turns out to be either a special challenge or a special interest in your family.

RESEARCH JOURNALS LIKELY AREN'T YOUR BEST FIRST STOP. As someone who has spent thousands of hours reading hundreds of academic journal articles for the last decade, I can say with certainty that parents don't have to dive headlong into *Reading Research Quarterly*, *Review of Educational Research*, or *Scientific Studies of Reading*. Ninety-nine percent of what's found there is not for us. That is, it's the work of scientists writing for scientists, not the public.

Peer-reviewed articles tend to be thick with jargon, statistical analysis, and theoretical concerns that are tough for a layperson to digest.

More than that, much of it is preliminary and inconclusive and therefore not helpful to your immediate project of raising a strong reader and writer. The scholars are publishing their findings not because they are definitive, but because they add to the body of knowledge on a topic by affirming or discrediting other theories or raising areas ripe for further research. Once they are published, more scholars can then weigh in on the rigor of their methods, the persuasiveness of their findings, and their relationship to other relevant studies.

EXPERTS DO DISSEMINATE INFORMATION DIRECTLY TO THE PUBLIC. Scott published in *The Conversation*, a publication that I first learned of when I took part in the OpEd Project's Public Voices program at the University of Texas, which trains underrepresented expert voices to enter public dialogue on critical subjects. During that program, I witnessed professors take great pains to break out of the jargon and conventions of their disciplines to deliver powerful, practical insights to a broad audience.

Some researchers also publish blogs and newsletters in which they share tips and tools for teachers and parents. I read posts on ShanahanOnLiteracy.com every week because its author, Timothy Shanahan, is a respected literacy expert who translates research and offers practical guidance to help teachers help students boost their reading achievement. He's taught first grade, written or edited two hundred literacy education articles, and chaired major federal reading-research review panels. The vast majority of his blog posts don't directly relate to what I'm experiencing with my own daughter, but reading them, observing how he evaluates research's quality and relevance, and following his logic teaches me a great deal about how to assess the content that flows my way.

Other ways to hear directly from experts include watching online recordings of their speeches and presentations, taking courses that they offer to teachers or parents, viewing documentaries that feature their work, and reading the guides and books they've published for parents, often in conjunction with research centers at their universities or national early-literacy nonprofits. Visit readingforour lives.com/experts for a roundup of resources featuring my favorite thinkers on early language and literacy.

Pay It Forward

After engaging with helpful research findings and getting familiar with research methods, you may be more open to *becoming* research. That is, taking part in an experiment or study meant to advance knowledge of language, learning, and child development. Such vital research requires real children and families to take part. Every one of the participants included in research methodology sections was recruited into the study by a researcher aiming to test a hypothesis.

And researchers struggle mightily to get families in on the action. Recruitment methods include mailings, phone calls, outreach through community organizations and churches, and even social media marketing. Enrollment woes often lead to smaller, more homogeneous participant groups and to less generalizable findings. The more diverse the base of willing participants, the more representative the findings can be. That's a realization that many have been slow to appreciate.

Lisa Oakes, a professor of psychology at the University of California, Davis, writes compellingly about an aha moment she had watching the documentary *Babies* by Thomas Balmès, when she observed extreme differences in the visual input received by an infant in Namibia compared with a baby in Tokyo.

"As depicted in the film, Ponijao had ample opportunity to look off in the distance, viewing the horizon, far-off trees, and people who emerged as tiny specks and became larger as they approached," she wrote, describing the infant in Namibia. "When Mari, in contrast, looked out the window of her apartment, she was surrounded by high-rise buildings directly in front of her. She saw trees in parks, of course, but never on the horizon. Although it used to seem implausible that race or ethnicity could influence basic processes like attention and memory, it now seemed quite plausible that a wide range of variables I have always ignored may play an important role in the development of even the most basic processes."

She'd been researching basic infant cognitive processes since 1991 in Iowa City, Iowa, an "overwhelmingly white" college town. She used babies from white, highly educated families as the subject of her research because it was convenient and she didn't think race or ethnicity had much to do with infant vision, memory, and attention. She thought her findings were generalizable. In fact, there are real differences in the environments and experiences of even the youngest children, and research must take them into account.

Even in cases when researchers intentionally recruit diverse participants, it's often hard to retain the subjects through the course of the project for all kinds of reasons—the time commitment required, distance from home, how and when they were asked to participate, language barriers, or the cultural sensitivity of the investigator.

I spoke with a researcher who had failed to complete an important study of the early impact of introducing children to faces from other races because most of the black families in the study (understandably) didn't want to read books with a bunch of white faces to their children. The researcher's request flew in the face of strongly held beliefs the black parents had about the importance of their kids seeing faces like their own in books to build a healthy sense of belonging, confidence, and worthiness.

The researcher will have to find another way to test her hypothesis. When she does, perhaps you'll participate?

Use GPS

After reading this book, you have a wealth of knowledge to tap into as you support your child, but don't stop here. Use what I nicknamed the "GPS framework" to keep the insights and informed decision-making going as your child grows or you encounter challenges beyond the scope of this book. It helps you put all kinds of reading information into proper context by considering three things: established guidelines, personal experience, and the wisdom of specialists.

When you're feeling stuck, overwhelmed, or confused at any point on this years-long journey, use this GPS combination to find your way. Literally, stop and take a moment to assess what's going on with your child. Consider their age and/or grade and then ground yourself in credible reference material, such as developmental milestone **guidelines** or kindergarten readiness checklists or state learning standards. Take some time to write out some **personal** thoughts and observations about your child in the moment, relative to what you've read. Then consult with a **specialist** in the relevant area to help you advance your understanding. Visit readingforourlives.com /gps to download a printable GPS worksheet that will walk you through the process, create space for self-reflections, and direct you to helpful child development guidance.

Guidelines. Well-researched lists of developmental milestones, school readiness checklists, and grade-level learning standards succinctly distill the best thinking on what to expect of kids when. Look to trusted sources, including the Centers for Disease Control, the National Institutes of Health, the American Academy of Pediatrics, and the National Association for the Education of Young Children for helpful distillation of research findings. Keep in mind that these sources provide useful perspective on typical development—not an ideal path, but *an average of many paths*.

Personal experience. You bring considerable knowledge and expertise to the table, and it's maximized when you consciously observe your child and your home, purposefully documenting what you see, hear, and experience. Pay attention to the gut feelings, recurring worries, or even feelings of calm and positivity that are all part of daily life with kids. Write down your observations. List your questions. Journal about what you've learned and discovered. You can collect all these thoughts in a paper journal on your nightstand as recommended in Chapter 2 or in a notes app on your phone—whatever method is most convenient for you. (Layer in some additional reminders to help you cement the habit, too, whether digital or analog. The best choice between a recurring weekly reminder on your calendar and a Post-it note on your mirror is the prompt you're most likely to notice and act on.)

Journaling, however informal, encourages greater self-awareness and self-knowledge, as well as better attention and attunement to your child's journey—not to mention a helpful record of your child's milestones and challenges to share with your village when needed.

Specialist insights. Now, once you're coming from a place of basic knowledge and awareness, if you sense there's an issue in your child's development or you just want to learn more, tap into other people who can help. Sometimes this requires you to expand your network or venture outside your comfort zone. Ask your pediatrician about the milestone or bring the topic up in a parents' group. This third step of reaching out, asking questions, and raising issues is critical. It sparks the habit of engaging with others around parenting, counteracts feelings of loneliness, and lessens worries about outside judgment.

All the GPS framework does is codify three steps that many savvy parents already think to do *sometimes*—so that you're more likely to repeat them again and again through your parenting years, as you face all manner of challenges, decisions, and issues. You can still consult family and friends, your media of choice, or Google. You'll just also have a handy prompt to ground your thinking in generally accepted milestones and standards; deep reflection on your child, your family, your aims; and the specific expertise of people working in the space.

One mom I spoke to noticed that her son was below age expectations in speech starting at his 9-month doctor's visit and began monitoring the situation closely. She brought up the issue with his pediatrician and, when he was still behind at 12 months, got a referral to free speech therapy through their county in Colorado.

"For me, taking my own concerns seriously and bringing them up with the pediatrician was key. Then the paperwork to get the evaluation took a while, but I tried to stay on top of that," she explained. "I also think looping in experts does help in this case. We heard a lot of well-meaning family and friends say, 'So-and-so's kid didn't talk at all until she was three, and now she never stops talking' or 'All second children talk late.' Those can be true, but it was also true in our case that our son had a developmental delay that is about more than just words, but about how he communicates with us."

And as you know, from reading this book, it's also about his long-term literacy prospects, because oral-language development is so intimately tied to vocabulary, comprehension, and the language of reading instruction.

―――――――――JOURNAL PROMPTS―――――――――

- What will your go-to sources for information on raising a reader be? Do some research and then list the specific websites, newsletters, or publications you intend to follow, including those listed in this chapter that resonated with you.

- How can you find early-childhood and -literacy organizations in your state or local community? What are the key criteria you will use to assess the quality of news and information about reading that you find in your chosen sources?

- How will you keep all the resources and organizations you discover top of mind? List specific actions like bookmarking their websites, subscribing to their newsletters, following their social media feeds, and so on.

Raising All Readers

Human rights are not things that are put on the table for people to enjoy. These are things you fight for and then you protect.
—Wangari Maathai

It's easy to lose sight of the big picture of your child's journey to reading, writing, and spelling because there's so much learning happening linguistically, cognitively, physically, and socioemotionally along the way. There are babbles and first words, scribbles and writing, letter-sound matches made, and words and sentences read—and understood.

You now have a number of ideas for educating yourself so that you can positively influence your child's literacy trajectory from day one. I've emphasized that there are critical milestones on the road to reading success and mapped the early-literacy terrain to help you gain a deeper, more nuanced understanding of what kids need and how you can provide or facilitate it.

Chapter 1 introduced you to your greatest raise-a-reader superpowers. Chapter 2 showed you what reading development from infancy to early elementary school looks like from the child's perspective. Chapter 3 outlined some enduring teaching principles to help you stay the course. Chapters 4 through 9 showed you how to spur key reading leaps, including boosting oral vocabulary, discerning sounds in words, grasping the form and function of print, mastering letters, mapping print to sound, and making meaning of it all. And Chapter 10 offered tips for learning as you go. I dug into each topic one by one to help you identify what to do, when, and (most important) how in everyday life with young children.

My hope is that together these chapters illustrate how prioritizing raising a reader gives you something meaningful around which to build your family life. That focus alone will alleviate a host of issues plaguing parents today—struggles to prioritize time and spending, lack of the knowledge and networks to make sound decisions, and failure to get the results you want despite lots of activity. That clarity of purpose also helps you attract the information, people, resources, and experiences you need.

It's impossible to teach your child everything they need to know to thrive in an unpredictable world. But when you focus on reading, you can rest assured that you're building the skill that supports all others. It truly facilitates learning in every other area of life— academically and personally, as workers and as citizens—and is the undisputed best tool to help kids meet the demands of adulthood. It's also a powerful bridge to the best of public life—libraries, schools, and community.

So much of the boredom and monotony that parents complain of in the first years of caregiving comes from our lack of knowledge about all the glorious development that's unfolding for our children. We can sometimes be inattentive and insensitive to the miracle in front of us. But when we know what we're observing, imagine what the child is experiencing, and aim to be responsive, our curiosity, attunement, and enjoyment of parenting grows.

I've endeavored to show you the breadth of your role in your child's life, the depth of their literacy needs, and the insufficiency of school alone to meet them. I hope that you will take what you've learned here and be a voice for good sense, good reason, and good instruction in your local community.

You can become an early-literacy expert in the time it takes to learn and grow in supporting your child's reading journey. You can become the smart voice for change in childcare settings and in schools. You can be the hands and heart that organizes the neighborhood book swap, hosts a toddler talk play group in your backyard, or advocates for everyday literacy wherever you go. You can be the public servant arguing for equity on the PTA, school board, or state legislature.

This isn't everyone's path, as Casey Stockstill, a mom of two and sociology professor at the University of Denver who studies preschool segregation, reminded me. "A lot of parents are having a mental health crisis right now, can't keep food on the table, or are just stressed to the max," she explains. "I think if you're in that spot, trying to parent your own kid with dignity is an activist move. That is amazing and that's the best thing to do."

But if you've found the time to read this book, you are likely a parent with the knowledge and ability to make a difference. You just have to decide to make your mission bigger than securing every advantage for your own child. "Parents and non-parents should think of the children in your community as everyone's children to some extent," Stockstill says. "We should care about how they're doing, because they're young and they don't have a lot of power yet. They need us to care about them."

———

I will never meet the person who inspired me to make advocating for children and families my life's work. She died in 1900 but left a legacy of conviction and quiet service that spoke to me powerfully, mother to mother, across centuries, in the months right after my first child was born.

Her name was Lucy Goode Brooks. I walked into Friends Association for Children, the latest iteration of the institution she built, 140 years after she established it. Enslaved in Virginia, Brooks gave birth to nine children and endured the aching tragedy of losing her eldest daughter twice: first to a cruel sale to a distant plantation and then to death in 1862.

When Emancipation dawned, it brought new sorrows and dislocations for Brooks, who watched the streets of Richmond, Virginia, fill with wandering, homeless children. The orphans were "free" but severed from their families by the chaos and cruelty of slavery and war. They reminded her of the child she'd lost, and she set about making a home for them, establishing Friends' Asylum for Colored Orphans in 1868 with the help of her Ladies' Sewing Circle and a Quaker benefactor.

In the years after Brooks's death, the orphanage morphed into a foster-home placement center for abused and neglected children, then into the early-childhood development center that I visited. Nearly a century and a half after she founded it, I toured the center on a site visit for a women's philanthropic group, in a world that would be in some ways unrecognizable to Brooks and in other ways all too familiar.

Walking its halls as a new mom, I felt at a gut level the unfairness of the world. My daughter had been born into a wealthy, educated household where no time, attention, or resources would be spared to give her every opportunity to live her best life, while across town other children just as worthy of living theirs faced much longer odds.

So I committed then and there to do my best to spread the word about things that really move the needle for kids and to continually empower myself and others to pursue them. This book is a pivotal part of that mission. May we all move with intention and collective power to raise our readers well—which is to say *all* readers.

How to Assess Childcare Providers and Schools from an Early-Literacy Perspective

While this book focuses on six things parents can do to build early literacy, it's also critical to ensure that the other teachers and caregivers in your child's life support your little one's language and literacy development. I've compiled a short bonus chapter to give you pointers on what to look for (and ask for) from those who help you care for your child.

Download this chapter at readingforourlives.com/caregivers.

Multimedia Resources

Thank you so much for reading this book. It was a great challenge and honor to assemble helpful resources for caregivers in the thick of raising readers. In addition, I've created some online tutorials and bonus materials to help illustrate points made within these pages. For example, audio provides the best example of how to pronounce English's forty-four phonemes, and video demonstrates conversational turns more vividly than text on a page. To access the book's multimedia and the printable worksheets referenced within chapters, visit www.readingforourlives.com.

Acknowledgments

Reading for Our Lives has been a lifetime in the making, and I owe a debt of gratitude to countless people who've helped me along the way. First and foremost, I thank my parents, the late James Edward Payne and Margaret Ralston Payne, who set my literacy trajectory sky-high with the love, talk, and care that they gave me from day one. I shared my last moments with my dad in the introduction of this book, and my mom's support has been just as essential. She encourages me daily with her faith, philanthropy, and service. I set out to write a book that's as smart, practical, and bighearted as she is.

My daughter, Zora, and husband, Shaka, are the MVPs in my life and work. With their words and examples, this dynamic duo inspires me to keep pushing, growing, and working toward the best version of myself. They are an endless fount of love, laughter, and accountability. I'm a more dedicated, more empathetic writer because of them. This book is a family project. We did it!

The influence of many mentors, colleagues, and friends bears on this project as well. My godmother, Genna Rae McNeil, has been a lifelong model of writing with integrity, courage, and power. Keffrelyn Brown affirmed the value of my mission and urged me to stay the course. Daina Ramey Berry taught me the brass tacks of file organization, chapter-by-chapter focus, and early morning check-ins. Nancy Redd offered a bright, cheerful example of and sounding board for juggling the joys and absurdities of writing, marriage, and motherhood. Joy Fuller was the best friend to call when the writing day was done—hours of long-distance hilarity ensued throughout this journey to publication.

Shout-out to my James River Writers and lit salon members in Richmond, Virginia—Kristin, Meg, Gigi, Stacy, Robin, Anne, Ellen, Ginny, Irene, Patty, and Laura—and my Writers' League of Texas, Texas Book Festival, and book people in Austin—Lise, Aisha, Maya P., Dalia, Suzanne, Becka, Heidi, Lois, Claire, Betsy, Clay, and Marc. You've all been constant reminders to hold fast to the author dream and the beauty of literary community.

Special thanks go to Ryan Holiday, who believed in this book and introduced me to my literary agent—the incomparable Lisa DiMona. I am indebted to Lisa for immediately grasping my raise-a-reader vision and responding to all of my questions with care and clarity. My deepest thanks for shepherding this project to a wonderful home at Avery and Penguin Random House, where I've been honored to work with a phenomenal team including Megan Newman, Nina Shield, Hannah Steigmeyer, Anne Kosmoski, Katie Macleod-English, Lindsay Gordon, Sara Johnson, Roshe Anderson, Marlena Brown, Nellys Liang, Amy Schneider, Claire Sullivan, and Melissa Mok.

Distilling high-quality academic research into accessible advice for parents was an incredible challenge for me as a journalist and first-time author. Writing coaches Jennie Nash, Shari Caudron, and Laraine Herring delivered invaluable reassurance and expert cheerleading in the early stages of planning and writing this book. And Andrea Rommel, fact-checker extraordinaire, brought greater precision to my analysis of studies and rigor to my recommendations. I can't thank her enough for the education she gave me in the manuscript margins. Thanks also to Jill Weisberg and Jennifer Borgioli Binis, who reviewed portions of this work.

The countless researchers, reporters, and practitioners whose efforts I reference in this book deserve credit, too. Thank you for sharing your work so that others might engage with your ideas and find guidance within them. I would like to thank Mary Ellen Isaacs, Jason Anthony, and Jill Gilkerson by name for deeply influencing my ideas about how children learn and thrive.

I must also acknowledge Susan Thacker-Gwaltney, who taught the Foundations of Reading Instruction course at the University of Virginia that first sent me endnote diving, and Lorraine Haricombe, vice provost and director of the University of Texas Libraries, whose leadership in library transformation and open-access educational resources took my learning and investigation in fresh directions. Hat tip to the many stellar educators in the Akron Public Schools, Harvard University, and the Medill School at Northwestern University whose lessons in curiosity, creativity, and care stuck with me.

I relocated to Milwaukee during the final months of writing this book and am so grateful for the warm reception that I received from Marquette University colleagues Heidi Bostic, Jody Jessup-Anger, and Leigh van den Kieboom in the College of Education and Sarah Feldner in the Diederich College of Communication. Howard Fuller, Ann McClain Terrell, Thelma Sias, Dea Wright, Wanda Montgomery, and Joan Johnson have also enthusiastically embraced my literacy work here. I am so excited to see how we collaborate to expand early educational opportunity for children in Milwaukee and beyond.

Endless gratitude goes to my MayaSmart.com team. Laila Weir has edited nearly every blog post, speech, op-ed, and article I've written in the last fifteen years. This book is better for the ways she's refined my thinking and writing. Kaara Kallen read this manuscript with her parent hat on to help me speak directly to the urgent needs of caregivers in the thick of raising readers. Courtney Runn, Kevin McClendon, and Kely Azevedo expertly managed my website and newsletter, which allowed me to keep pen to paper on longer-form projects. It's no understatement to say that I couldn't bring this work to light without my team.

Finally, thanks to my website visitors, newsletter subscribers, VIP (Very Intentional Parent) community, and you, dear reader, for allowing me to learn and share alongside you on the caregiver journey.

Notes

By necessity, by proclivity, and by delight, we all quote.
—Ralph Waldo Emerson

I interviewed a number of experts and consulted a wide array of documents and reports across disciplines from neuroscience, history, and linguistics to psychology, education, and speech therapy. I've included a detailed list of citations here for those who would like to check my work or expand upon it. Inevitably, there are additions and corrections that don't make it into print. If you discover relevant references or attributions, please email me at hello@mayasmart.com so I can set the record straight. A book like this is only as helpful as the sources it relies on, so suggestions for improvements are always welcome.

You can find an updated list of endnotes and amendments at readingforourlives.com/endnotes.

INTRODUCTION

1. **basic skills are weak overall:** OECD (2013), *Time for the U.S. to Reskill?: What the Survey of Adult Skills Says* (OECD Skills Studies, OECD Publishing), 3, 11–12.
1. **unusually persistent across generations:** OECD (2013), *Time for the U.S. to Reskill?*, 3, 11–12.
2. **one in six U.S. adults has low literacy skills:** OECD (2013), *Time for the U.S. to Reskill?*, 11.
2. **36 million U.S. adults:** OECD (2013), *Time for the U.S. to Reskill?*, 33.
2. **can't compare and contrast:** OECD (2013), *Time for the U.S. to Reskill?*, 61.
2. **more likely to pass on weaker skills:** OECD (2013), *Time for the U.S. to Reskill?*, 32–33.

2. **likelihood of incarceration:** *Highlights from the U.S. PIAAC Survey of Incarcerated Adults: Their Skills, Work Experience, Education, and Training* (2016), 5, https://nces.ed.gov /pubs2016/2016040.pdf.

2. **more than a million new neural connections:** Center on the Developing Child at Harvard University, "Brain Architecture," https://developingchild.harvard.edu/science/key-concepts /brain-architecture; Pat Levitt and Kathie L. Eagleson, "The Ingredients of Healthy Brain and Child Development Bringing Science to Law and Policy," *Washington University Journal of Law & Policy* 57 (2018): 79, https://openscholarship.wustl.edu/cgi/viewcontent.cgi?article =2052&context=law_journal_law_policy.

2. **in place by around 2 years old:** John H. Gilmore, Rebecca C. Knickmeyer, and Wei Gao, "Imaging Structural and Functional Brain Development in Early Childhood," *Nature Reviews Neuroscience* 19, no. 3 (March 1, 2018): 123, https://doi.org/10.1038/nrn.2018.1.

2. **stimulates brain function and shapes brain structure:** Rachel R. Romeo et al., "Beyond the 30-Million-Word Gap: Children's Conversational Exposure Is Associated with Language-Related Brain Function," *Psychological Science* 29, no. 5 (2018): 700–710, https:// doi.org/10.1177/0956797617742725; Rianne Kok et al., "Normal Variation in Early Parental Sensitivity Predicts Child Structural Brain Development," *Journal of the American Academy of Child and Adolescent Psychiatry* 54, no. 10 (2015): 824–831, https://doi.org/10.1016 /j.jaac.2015.07.009; Vaheshta Sethna et al., "Mother–Infant Interactions and Regional Brain Volumes in Infancy: An MRI Study," *Brain Structure and Function* 222 (2017): 2379–2388, https://doi.org/10.1007/s00429-016-1347-1; A. Rifkin-Graboi et al., "Maternal Sensitivity, Infant Limbic Structure Volume and Functional Connectivity: A Preliminary Study," *Translational Psychiatry* 5 (2015): e668, https://doi.org/10.1038/tp.2015.133.

3. **"significantly lower" emergent literacy:** OECD, *Early Learning and Child Well-Being: A Study of Five-Year-Olds in England, Estonia, and the United States* (Paris: OECD Publishing, 2020), https://doi.org/10.1787/3990407f-en.

3. **one-third of a nationally representative sample:** National Center for Education Statistics, "NAEP Report Card: 2019 NAEP Reading Assessment," https://www.nationsreportcard .gov/highlights/reading/2019.

3. **9- and 13-year-olds have dropped:** National Center for Education Statistics, "NAEP Report Card: NAEP Long-Term Trend Assessment Results: Reading and Mathematics," https://www.nationsreportcard.gov/ltt/reading/student-experiences/?age=13.

3. **14 percent of U.S. 15-year-olds read well enough:** OECD, *Country Note United States: Programme for International Student Assessment (PISA) Results from PISA 2018*, 3, https:// www.oecd.org/pisa/publications/PISA2018_CN_USA.pdf; OECD, *21st-Century Readers: Developing Literacy Skills in a Digital World* (Paris: PISA, OECD Publishing, 2021), https:// doi.org/10.1787/a83d84cb-en.

3. **"never or hardly ever" read for fun:** National Center for Education Statistics, "NAEP Report Card: NAEP Long-Term Trend Assessment Results: Reading and Mathematics," https://www.nationsreportcard.gov/ltt/reading/student-experiences/?age=13.

4. **30 percent of instructional time:** Soheyla Taie, Rebecca Goldring, and Maura Spiegelman, *Characteristics of Public and Private Elementary and Secondary Schools in the United States: Results from the 2017–18 National Teacher and Principal Survey. First Look. NCES 2019-140* (Washington, DC: National Center for Education Statistics, August 2019), 19, https://nces .ed.gov/pubsearch/pubsinfo.asp?pubid=2019140; Ina V. S. Mullis et al., *PIRLS 2016: International Results in Reading* (Chestnut Hill, MA: TIMSS & PIRLS International Study Center, Lynch School of Education, Boston College, and International Association for the Evaluation of Educational Achievement, 2017), 256, http://pirls2016.org/wp-content /uploads/structure/CompletePDF/P16-PIRLS-International-Results-in-Reading.pdf; Geoffrey Phelps et al., "How Much English Language Arts and Mathematics Instruction Do Students

Receive? Investigating Variation in Instructional Time," *Educational Policy* 26, no. 5 (2012): 647–648, https://doi.org/10.1177/0895904811417580; Tina L. Heafner and Paul G. Fitchett, "Tipping the Scales: National Trends of Declining Social Studies Instructional Time in Elementary Schools," *The Journal of Social Studies Research* 36, no. 2 (2012): 199–200.

7. **"the world and the heavens"**: Zora Neale Hurston, *Their Eyes Were Watching God* (New York: Perennial Library, 1990), 72.

7. **Jabari Asim's *Girl of Mine***: Jabari Asim, *Girl of Mine* (New York: LB Kids, 2010).

7. **"We die. That may be the meaning of life"**: Toni Morrison, Nobel Lecture, December 7, 1993, https://www.nobelprize.org/prizes/literature/1993/morrison/lecture.

8. **the brain is at its most flexible**: Center on the Developing Child at Harvard University, "InBrief: The Science of Early Childhood Development," 2007, https://developingchild .harvard.edu/resources/inbrief-science-of-ecd.

11. **predicted their IQ and language skills *ten years later***: Jill Gilkerson et al., "Language Experience in the Second Year of Life and Language Outcomes in Late Childhood," *Pediatrics* 142, no. 4 (October 1, 2018): 5–8, https://doi.org/10.1542/peds.2017-4276.

11. **growing distractions**: Brooke Auxier et al., *Parenting Children in the Age of Screens* (Washington, DC: Pew Research Center, July 2020), 11–12, 47–49, 53–62, https://www .pewresearch.org/internet/wp-content/uploads/sites/9/2020/07/PI_2020.07.28_kids-and -screens_FINAL.pdf; Laura Bornfreund et al., *Supporting Early Learning in America: Policies for a New Decade* (Washington, DC: New America, February 2020), 7–11, https:// d1y8sb8igg2f8e.cloudfront.net/documents/Supporting_Early_Learning_in_America _FINAL_JZxpW0v.pdf; Jack Cassidy, Evan Ortlieb, and Stephanie Grote-Garcia, "What's Hot in Literacy: New Topics and New Frontiers Are Abuzz," *Literacy Research and Instruction* 60, no. 1 (2020): 4, https://doi.org/10.1080/19388071.2020.1800202; Common Sense Media, "New Report: Parents Spend More Than Nine Hours a Day with Screen Media," press release, December 6, 2016, https://www.commonsensemedia.org/about-us/news /press-releases/new-report-parents-spend-more-than-nine-hours-a-day-with-screen-media; The Genius of Play, "When It Comes to Screen Time, Parents Are Just as Guilty as Their Children," press release, October 21, 2019, https://www.prnewswire.com/news-releases /when-it-comes-to-screen-time-parents-are-just-as-guilty-as-their-children-300941553 .html.

11. **single best predictor of school achievement**: Amy Pace et al., "Measuring Success: Within and Cross-Domain Predictors of Academic and Social Trajectories in Elementary School," *Early Childhood Research Quarterly* 46 (January 1, 2019): 112–125, https://doi.org/10.1016 /j.ecresq.2018.04.001.

11. **four times as likely to drop out:** Donald J. Hernandez, *Double Jeopardy: How Third Grade Reading Skills and Poverty Influence High School Graduation* (Baltimore: The Annie E. Casey Foundation, January 2012), https://www.aecf.org/resources/double-jeopardy.

11. **usually had no effect on reading achievement**: Beth Boulay et al., *Summary of Research Generated by Striving Readers on the Effectiveness of Interventions for Struggling Adolescent Readers* (Washington, DC: National Center for Education Evaluation and Regional Assistance, Institute of Education Sciences, U.S. Department of Education, October 2015), 1–8, https://ies.ed.gov/ncee/pubs/20164001/pdf/20164001.pdf; Rekha Balu et al., *Evaluation of Response to Intervention Practices for Elementary School Reading* (Washington, DC: National Center for Education Evaluation and Regional Assistance, Institute of Education Sciences, U.S. Department of Education, November 2015), 87–94, https://ies .ed.gov/ncee/pubs/20164000/pdf/20164000.pdf; Timothy Shanahan, *Shanahan on Literacy* (blog), "How Much Reading Gain Should Be Expected from Reading Interventions?," February 13, 2017, Reading Rockets, https://www.readingrockets.org/blogs/shanahan -literacy/how-much-reading-gain-should-be-expected-reading-interventions.

12. **levels of reading and writing required:** Donald J. Leu et al., "New Literacies: A Dual-Level Theory of the Changing Nature of Literacy, Instruction, and Assessment," *Journal of Education* 197, no. 2 (2017): 1–3, https://doi.org/10.1177/002205741719700202; Richard Murnane, Isabel Sawhill, and Catherine Snow, "Literacy Challenges for the Twenty-First Century: Introducing the Issue," *Future of Children* 22, no. 2 (Fall 2012): 3–10, https://doi .org/10.1353/foc.2012.0013; OECD, *Literacy in the Information Age: Final Report of the International Adult Literacy Survey* (Paris: OECD and the Minister of Industry, Canada, 2000), 1–11, https://www.oecd.org/education/skills-beyond-school/41529765.pdf.

13. **100,000 studies on how children learn to read:** Eunice Kennedy Shriver National Institute of Child Health and Human Development, NIH, DHHS, Child Development and Behavior Branch, *Report of the National Reading Panel, Teaching Children to Read: An Evidence-Based Assessment of the Scientific Research Literature on Reading and Its Implications for Reading Instruction* (Washington, DC: U.S. Government Printing Office, 2000), https://www.nichd.nih.gov/publications/pubs/nrp/intro.

15. **"resist the urge to engage in reading instruction":** Daniel T. Willingham, *Raising Kids Who Read: What Parents and Teachers Can Do* (San Francisco: Jossey-Bass/Wiley, 2015), 93.

1. BEYOND BEDTIME STORIES: THE TRUTH ABOUT GETTING KIDS READY TO READ

19. **"Young kids whose parents read":** Virginia Sole-Smith, "How to Raise a Child Who Loves to Read," *Parents*, August 2020, https://www.parents.com/toddlers-preschoolers /development/reading/how-to-raise-a-reader.

20. **"the single most significant factor":** "Read 3 Pledge," H-E-B, https://www.heb.com /static-page/Read-3-Pledge.

20. **"The rewards of early reading":** Meghan Cox Gurdon, *The Enchanted Hour: The Miraculous Power of Reading Aloud in the Age of Distraction* (New York: HarperCollins, 2019), xiv.

21. **"Without a concerted look":** Dana Suskind, *Thirty Million Words: Building a Child's Brain* (New York: Dutton, 2015), 225.

21. **cognitive function disparities:** Marianne M. Hillemeier et al., "Disparities in the Prevalence of Cognitive Delay: How Early Do They Appear?," *Paediatric and Perinatal Epidemiology* 23, no. 3 (May 2009): 186–198, https://doi.org/10.1111/j.1365-3016.2008.01006.x.

21. **language processing gaps:** Anne Fernald, Virginia A. Marchman, and Adriana Weisleder, "SES Differences in Language Processing Skill and Vocabulary Are Evident at 18 Months," *Developmental Science* 16, no. 2 (2013): 239–242, https://doi.org/10.1111/desc.12019; Kimberly G. Noble et al., "Socioeconomic Disparities in Neurocognitive Development in the First Two Years of Life," *Developmental Psychobiology* 57, no. 5 (2015): 535–551, https:// doi.org/10.1002/dev.21303.

22. **Early talk is our point of greatest leverage:** LENA, *Inside Early Talk* (Boulder, CO: LENA Foundation, March 2021), 17, https://info.lena.org/inside-early-talk.

22. **back-and-forth dialogue with adults:** Jill Gilkerson et al., "Language Experience in the Second Year of Life and Language Outcomes in Late Childhood," *Pediatrics* 142, no. 4 (October 1, 2018): 5–8, https://doi.org/10.1542/peds.2017-4276.

22. **significantly higher IQ and better language skills as adolescents:** Gilkerson et al., "Language Experience."

22. **talkative toddlers with talkative parents:** Gilkerson et al., "Language Experience," 5–8.

23. **the greater the activity in their Broca's area:** Rachel R. Romeo et al., "Beyond the 30-Million-Word Gap: Children's Conversational Exposure Is Associated with Language-Related Brain Function," *Psychological Science* 29, no. 5 (May 1, 2018): 700–710, https://doi .org/10.1177/0956797617742725.

23. **affect language processing:** Romeo et al., "Beyond the 30-Million-Word Gap."

23. **change the *physical structure* of the brain:** Rachel R. Romeo et al., "Language Exposure Relates to Structural Neural Connectivity in Childhood," *Journal of Neuroscience* 38, no. 36 (September 5, 2018): 7870–7877, https://doi.org/10.1523/JNEUROSCI.0484-18.2018.

23. **drive parents to chronic distraction:** Erika Christakis, "The Dangers of Distracted Parenting," *The Atlantic*, July/August 2018, https://www.theatlantic.com/magazine/archive/2018/07/the-dangers-of-distracted-parenting/561752.

23. **IQ, listening comprehension, and vocabulary:** Gilkerson et al., "Language Experience."

23. **overall language ability:** Rachel I. Mayberry, Alex A. del Giudice, and Amy M. Lieberman, "Reading Achievement in Relation to Phonological Coding and Awareness in Deaf Readers: A Meta-analysis," *Journal of Deaf Studies and Deaf Education* 16, no. 2 (2010): 164–188, https://academic.oup.com/jdsde/article/16/2/164/364821.

23. **its own syntax and grammar:** "American Sign Language," National Institute on Deafness and Other Communication Disorders, October 29, 2021, https://www.nidcd.nih.gov/health/american-sign-language.

23. **Skilled deaf signers are often better readers:** Carol Padden and Claire Ramsey, "American Sign Language and Reading Ability in Deaf Children," in *Language Acquisition by Eye*, eds. Charlene Chamberlain, Jill Morford, and Rachel Mayberry (Mahwah, NJ: Lawrence Erlbaum Associates, 2000), 221–259.

24. **no health professional:** Dana Suskind et al., "Educating Parents about Infant Language Development: A Randomized Controlled Trial," *Clinical Pediatrics* 57, no. 8 (2018): 947, https://doi.org/10.1177/0009922817737079.

24. **"the single most important activity":** Julie Dwyer and Susan B. Neuman, "Selecting Books for Children Birth through Four: A Developmental Approach," *Early Childhood Education Journal* 35, no. 6 (2008): 489, https://doi.org/10.1007/s10643-008-0236-5.

25. **more complex and novel words:** Jessica L. Montag, Michael N. Jones, and Linda B. Smith, "The Words Children Hear: Picture Books and the Statistics for Language Learning," *Psychological Science* 26, no. 9 (2015): 1489–96, https://doi.org/10.1177/0956797615594361.

26. **associated with better literacy, numeracy:** Joanna Sikora, M.D.R. Evans, and Jonathan Kelley, "Scholarly Culture: How Books in Adolescence Enhance Adult Literacy, Numeracy and Technology Skills in 31 Societies," *Social Science Research* 77 (2019): 5–14, https://doi.org/10.1016/j.ssresearch.2018.10.003.

26. **held across pooled data:** Sikora, Evans, and Kelley, "Scholarly Culture."

26. **"the benefits of bookishness":** Sikora, Evans, and Kelley, "Scholarly Culture."

27. **intentional, direct instruction:** Anne Castles, Kathleen Rastle, and Kate Nation, "Ending the Reading Wars: Reading Acquisition from Novice to Expert," *Psychological Science in the Public Interest* 19, no. 1 (June 1, 2018): 5–51, https://doi.org/10.1177/1529100618772271.

27. **make a word stick in memory:** Amanda Rawlins and Martha Invernizzi, "Reconceptualizing Sight Words: Building an Early Reading Vocabulary," *Reading Teacher* 72, no. 6 (2018): 714–716, https://doi.org/10.1002/trtr.1789.

29. **side by side with her:** Catherine Compton-Lilly and Anne Delbridge, "What Can Parents Tell Us about Poverty and Literacy Learning? Listening to Parents over Time," *Journal of Adolescent and Adult Literacy* 62, no. 5 (March/April 2019): 537, https://doi.org/10.1002/jaal.923.

32. **high-interest loan:** Highlite Education Loans, "Tutoring Financing & Education Loans," https://highliteloans.com.

32. **"explosion in demand" for preschool tutoring:** Douglas Belkin and Globe Staff, "Bringing Up Einstein: Tutor Businesses Tap into a Growing Market: Preschoolers," *Boston Globe*, February 19, 2006, 3rd ed., Globe NorthWest sec; Marek Fuchs, "Education: Tutoring Gives Pupils an Edge . . . for Preschool," *New York Times*, July 31, 2002, Metro sec., B9.

32. **boom at least through 2026:** Vlad Khaustovich, "Tutoring and Driving Schools in the US," IBISWorld, 2021.

32. **will need extra supports:** Allison H. Friedman-Krauss et al., *The State of Preschool 2020, State Preschool Yearbook*, National Institute for Early Education Research, 2021.
34. **NAEYC recommends:** "Principles of Effective Family Engagement," NAEYC, https://www .naeyc.org/resources/topics/family-engagement/principles.
36. **teach parents about local school issues:** "Family Leadership Institute," City Forward Collective, https://www.cityforwardcollective.org/family-leadership-institute.

2. THE LONG RUN: HOW TO NURTURE READING AT EACH AGE AND STAGE

40. **millions of years ago:** Rachel Gutman, "A 'Mic Drop' on a Theory of Language Evolution," *The Atlantic*, December 12, 2019, https://www.theatlantic.com /science/archive/2019/12/when-did-ancient-humans-start-speak/603484.
40. **most monolingual children:** "How Does Your Child Hear and Talk?," American Speech-Language-Hearing Association, https://www.asha.org/public/speech/development/chart.
41. **much more recently in human history:** Roger D. Woodard, "Writing Systems," in *International Encyclopedia of the Social and Behavioral Sciences (Second Edition)*, ed. James D. Wright (Oxford: Elsevier, 2015), 773–774, https://doi.org/10.1016/B978-0-08 -097086-8.52027-3.
41. **"recycling" of brain networks:** Stanislas Dehaene, "Evolution of Human Cortical Circuits for Reading and Arithmetic: The 'Neuronal Recycling' Hypothesis," in *From Monkey Brain to Human Brain: A Fyssen Foundation Symposium*, ed. Stanislas Dehaene, Jean-René Duhamel, Marc D. Hauser, and Giacomo Rizzolatti (Cambridge, MA: MIT Press, 2005), 141–151; Stanislas Dehaene and Laurent Cohen, "Cultural Recycling of Cortical Maps," *Neuron* 56, no. 2 (October 25, 2007): 384–390, https://doi.org/10.1016/j.neuron.2007.10.004.
42. **before birth:** Anthony J. DeCasper and Melanie J. Spence, "Prenatal Maternal Speech Influences Newborns' Perception of Speech Sounds," *Infant Behavior and Development* 9, no. 2 (April–June 1986): 134–148, https://doi.org/10.1016/0163-6383(86)90025-1; P. G. Hepper, D. Scott, and S. Shahidullah, "Newborn and Fetal Response to Maternal Voice," *Journal of Reproductive and Infant Psychology* 11, no. 3 (1993): 148–152, https://doi .org/10.1080/02646839308403210; B. S. Kisilevsky et al., "Fetal Sensitivity to Properties of Maternal Speech and Language," *Infant Behavior and Development* 32, no. 1 (January 2009): 59–68, https://doi.org/10.1016/j.infbeh.2008.10.002.
42. **By the third trimester of pregnancy:** Carolyn Granier-Deferre et al., "Near-Term Fetuses Process Temporal Features of Speech," *Developmental Science* 14, no. 2 (2011): 340–348, https://doi.org/10.1111/j.1467-7687.2010.00978.x.
42. **contributes to phonetic perception:** Christine Moon, Hugo Lagercrantz, and Patricia K. Kuhl, "Language Experienced *in Utero* Affects Vowel Perception after Birth: A Two-Country Study," *Acta Paediatrica* 102, no. 2 (February 2013): 156–159, https://doi.org/10.1111 /apa.12098.
42. **"vowels are louder":** Moon, Lagercrantz, and Kuhl, "Language Experienced," 156.
42. **reacted differently to vowel sounds:** Moon, Lagercrantz, and Kuhl, "Language Experienced," 158–159.
43. **"Crying is, in fact, nature's way":** Nicola Lathey and Tracey Blake, *Small Talk: How to Develop Your Child's Language Skills from Birth to Age 4* (New York: The Experiment, 2014), 36.
43. **third month of life:** Kathleen Wermke, "Neonatal Crying Behaviors," in International Encyclopedia of the Social and Behavorial Sciences (Second Edition), ed. James D. Wright (Oxford: Elsevier, 2015): 475, https://doi.org/10.1016/B978-0-08-097086-8.23106-1.
43. **between 2 and 4 months old:** B. D'Entremont, S. M. J. Hains, and D. W. Muir, "A Demonstration of Gaze Following in 3- to 6-Month-Olds," *Infant Behavior and Development* 20, no. 4 (October–December 1997): 569–571, https://doi.org/10.1016/S0163-6383(97) 90048-5; Gustaf Gredebäck, Linn Fikke, and Annika Melinder, "The Development of Joint

Visual Attention: A Longitudinal Study of Gaze Following during Interactions with Mothers and Strangers," *Developmental Science* 13, no. 6 (November 2010): 841–847, https://doi.org /10.1111/j.1467-7687.2009.00945.x; Melis Çetinçelik, Caroline F. Rowland, and Tineke M. Snijders, "Do the Eyes Have It? A Systematic Review on the Role of Eye Gaze in Infant Language Development," *Frontiers in Psychology* 11 (January 8, 2021): 3–12, https://doi.org /10.3389/fpsyg.2020.589096.

44. **By 6 months old:** Julie Dwyer and Susan B. Neuman, "Selecting Books for Children Birth Through Four: A Developmental Approach," *Early Childhood Education Journal* 35, (2008): 490, https://doi.org/10.1007/s10643-008-0236-5.

44. **right-fit visual and tactile stimulation:** Dwyer and Neuman, "Selecting Books for Children," 490–491.

44. **your baby is driving their own learning:** Jenny R. Saffran, "Statistical Language Learning in Infancy," *Child Development Perspectives* 14, no. 1 (2020): 49–543, https://doi.org/10.1111 /cdep.12355.

44. **"Your choice of books":** Caroline J. Blakemore and Barbara Weston Ramirez, *Baby Read-Aloud Basics: Fun and Interactive Ways to Help Your Little One Discover the World of Words* (New York: AMACOM, 2006), 28.

45. **better expressive and receptive language skills:** Amber Muhinyi and Meredith L. Rowe, "Shared Reading with Preverbal Infants and Later Language Development," *Journal of Applied Developmental Psychology* 64 (July–September 2019): 101053, 3–6, https://doi.org /10.1016/j.appdev.2019.101053.

47. **"all the ideas of a toddler":** Susie Allison (@busytoddler), "Shout out to everyone with a taby this summer," Instagram photo, July 13, 2021, https://www.instagram.com/p /CRRfy3IrXgL.

47. **bolster your little one's brain connectivity:** Rachel R. Romeo et al., "Language Exposure Relates to Structural Neural Connectivity in Childhood," *Journal of Neuroscience* 38, no. 36 (September 5, 2018): 7871–7876, https://doi.org/10.1523/JNEUROSCI.0484-18.2018; Rachel R. Romeo et al., "Neuroplasticity Associated with Changes in Conversational Turn-Taking Following a Family-Based Intervention," *Developmental Cognitive Neuroscience* 49 (June 2021): 100967, 2–9, https://doi.org/10.1016/j.dcn.2021.100967; Jill Gilkerson et al., "Language Experience in the Second Year of Life and Language Outcomes in Late Childhood," *Pediatrics* 142, no. 4 (October 2018): e20174276, 2–9, https://doi.org/10.1542 /peds.2017-4276.

47. **best predictor of expressive vocabulary:** Ed Donnellan et al., "Infants' Intentionally Communicative Vocalizations Elicit Responses from Caregivers and Are the Best Predictors of the Transition to Language: A Longitudinal Investigation of Infants' Vocalizations, Gestures and Word Production," *Developmental Science* 23, no. 1 (2020): e12843, https://doi .org/10.1111/desc.12843.

49. **may still get clipped:** Linda M. Laila Khan, "A Review of 16 Major Phonological Processes," *Language, Speech, and Hearing Services in Schools* 13, no. 2 (April 1982): 79–80, https://doi .org/10.1044/0161-1461.1302.77; "Selected Phonological Processes (Patterns)," American Speech-Language-Hearing Association, accessed February 3, 2022, https://www.asha.org /practice-portal/clinical-topics/articulation-and-phonology/selected-phonological-processes.

55. **increases the time 3-to-5-year-olds look at print:** Mary Ann Evans, Karen Williamson, and Tiffany Pursoo, "Preschoolers' Attention to Print During Shared Book Reading," *Scientific Studies of Reading* 12, no. 1 (January 21, 2008): 106–129, https://doi .org/10.1080/10888430701773884.

57. **A few quick definitions:** Linnea C. Ehri, "The Science of Learning to Read Words: A Case for Systematic Phonics Instruction," *Reading Research Quarterly* 55, no. S1 (2020): S45–S60, https://doi.org/10.1002/rrq.334.

3. YES YOU CAN: FIVE TOUCHSTONES FOR PARENTS WHO DARE TO TEACH

62. **affect kids' language development:** Meredith L. Rowe, "Understanding Socioeconomic Differences in Parents' Speech to Children," *Child Development Perspectives* 12, no. 2 (June 2018): 122–123, https://doi.org/10.1111/cdep.12271; Zehava Oz Weizman and Catherine E. Snow, "Lexical Output as Related to Children's Vocabulary Acquisition: Effects of Sophisticated Exposure and Support for Meaning," *Developmental Psychology* 37, no. 2 (2001), 265–279, https://doi.org/10.1037/0012-1649.37.2.265; Janellen Huttenlocher et al., "Sources of Variability in Children's Language Growth," *Cognitive Psychology* 61, no. 4 (December 1, 2010): 345–360, https://doi.org/10.1016/j.cogpsych.2010.08.002.

62. **parent responsiveness:** Catherine S. Tamis-LeMonda, Yana Kuchirko, and Lulu Song, "Why Is Infant Language Learning Facilitated by Parental Responsiveness?," *Current Directions in Psychological Science* 23, no. 2 (2014): 121–125, https://doi.org/10.1177/0963721414522813.

62. **"Reciprocal and dynamic interactions":** Jack P. Shonkoff, "Breakthrough Impacts: What Science Tells Us About Supporting Early Childhood Development," *YC Young Children* 72, no. 2 (2017): 9, http://www.jstor.org/stable/90004117.

63. **conversations about the here and now:** Michael Tomasello and Michael Jeffrey Farrar, "Joint Attention and Early Language," *Child Development* 57, no. 6 (December 1986): 1454–1460, https://doi.org/10.2307/1130423; Meredith L. Rowe and Susan Goldin-Meadow, "Differences in Early Gesture Explain SES Disparities in Child Vocabulary Size at School Entry," *Science* 323, no. 5916 (February 13, 2009): 951–953, https://doi.org/10.1126/science.1167025.

63. **advance infants' language learning:** Erik D. Thiessen, Emily A. Hill, and Jenny R. Saffran, "Infant-Directed Speech Facilitates Word Segmentation," *Infancy* 7, no. 1 (January 2005): 56–65, https://doi.org/10.1207/s15327078in0701_5; Nairán Ramírez-Esparza, Adrián García-Sierra, and Patricia K. Kuhl, "Look Who's Talking: Speech Style and Social Context in Language Input to Infants Are Linked to Concurrent and Future Speech Development," *Developmental Science* 17, no. 6 (2014): 882–889, https://doi.org/10.1111/desc.12172.

63. **evokes a response from babies:** Roberta Michnick Golinkoff et al., "(Baby)Talk to Me: The Social Context of Infant-Directed Speech and Its Effects on Early Language Acquisition," *Current Directions in Psychological Science* 24, no. 5 (2015): 339–343, https://doi.org/10.1177/0963721415595345.

63. **greater influence on kids' vocabulary growth:** Meredith L. Rowe, "A Longitudinal Investigation of the Role of Quantity and Quality of Child-Directed Speech in Vocabulary Development," *Child Development* 83, no. 5 (September/October 2012): 1764–1773, https://doi.org/10.1111/j.1467-8624.2012.01805.x.

63. **positively related to kids' vocabulary skill a year later:** Rowe, "A Longitudinal Investigation," 1764–1773.

64. **Numerous studies across the human life span:** Nicholas J. Cepeda et al., "Distributed Practice in Verbal Recall Tasks: A Review and Quantitative Synthesis," *Psychological Bulletin* 132, no. 3 (2006): 354–380, https://doi.org/10.1037/0033-2909.132.3.354.

64. **wide range of to-be-learned material:** Emilie Gerbier and Thomas C. Toppino, "The Effect of Distributed Practice: Neuroscience, Cognition, and Education," *Trends in Neuroscience and Education* 4, no. 3 (September 2015): 50, https://doi.org/10.1016/j.tine.2015.01.001.

64. **performed better:** Nancy J. Sullivan et al., "Simulation Exercise to Improve Retention of Cardiopulmonary Resuscitation Priorities for In-Hospital Cardiac Arrests: A Randomized Controlled Trial," *Resuscitation* 86 (January 1, 2015): 6–13, https://doi.org/10.1016/j.resuscitation.2014.10.021; Yiqun Lin et al., "Improving CPR Quality with Distributed Practice and Real-Time Feedback in Pediatric Healthcare Providers—A Randomized Controlled Trial," *Resuscitation* 130 (September 1, 2018): 6–12, https://doi.org/10.1016/j.resuscitation.2018.06.025.

64. **most replicated findings:** Haley A. Vlach, Catherine A. Bredemann, and Carla Kraft, "To Mass or Space? Young Children Do Not Possess Adults' Incorrect Biases about Spaced Learning," *Journal of Experimental Child Psychology* 183 (July 2019): 116, https://doi.org /10.1016/j.jecp.2019.02.003.

64. **a bias for massed learning:** Vlach, Bredemann, and Kraft, "To Mass or Space?," 118–132.

66. **levels of personal relevance:** Stacy J. Priniski, Cameron A. Hecht, and Judith M. Harackiewicz, "Making Learning Personally Meaningful: A New Framework for Relevance Research," *The Journal of Experimental Education* 86, no. 1 (2018): 12, https://doi.org /10.1080/00220973.2017.1380589.

66. **your demeanor, your engagement, and your responsiveness:** Susan Sonnenschein and Kimberly Munsterman, "The Influence of Home-Based Reading Interactions on 5-Year-Olds' Reading Motivations and Early Literacy Development," *Early Childhood Research Quarterly* 17, no. 3 (January 1, 2002): 323–335, https://doi.org/10.1016/S0885-2006(02)00167-9.

67. **Research by psychologist Carol Dweck and others:** Elizabeth A. Gunderson et al., "Parent Praise to Toddlers Predicts Fourth Grade Academic Achievement via Children's Incremental Mindsets," *Developmental Psychology* 54, no. 3 (March 2018): 398–405, https://doi.org /10.1037/dev0000444.

67. **a longitudinal study:** Gunderson et al., "Parent Praise," 398–407.

4. YOU'RE HIRED: ESSENTIAL LESSONS EVERY PARENT CAN—AND SHOULD— GIVE KIDS

71. **since the late fourth millennium BCE:** Roger D. Woodard, "Writing Systems," in *International Encyclopedia of the Social and Behavioral Sciences* (Second Edition), ed. James D. Wright (Oxford: Elsevier, 2015), 773–774, https://doi.org/10.1016/B978-0 -08-097086-8.52027-3.

71. **since the sixteenth century:** John Hart, *An Orthographie* (1569; London: Fred Pitman, 1850). Google Books.

71. **last several decades:** Keith Rayner et al., "How Psychological Science Informs the Teaching of Reading," *Psychological Science in the Public Interest* 2, no. 2 (November 2001): 34–68, https://doi.org/10.1111/1529-1006.00004.

72. **critically important for later reading skills:** Christopher J. Lonigan, Stephen R. Burgess, and Jason L. Anthony, "Development of Emergent Literacy and Early Reading Skills in Preschool Children: Evidence from a Latent-Variable Longitudinal Study," *Developmental Psychology* 36, no. 5 (2000): 598–610, https://doi.org/10.1037/0012-1649.36.5.596.

72. **preschool and kindergarten screenings:** Marcia Invernizzi et al., "Increased Implementation of Emergent Literacy Screening in Pre-Kindergarten," *Early Childhood Education Journal* 37 (2010): 437–445, https://doi.org/10.1007/s10643-009-0371-7; Maura Jones Moyle, John Heilmann, and S. Sue Berman, "Assessment of Early Developing Phonological Awareness Skills: A Comparison of the Preschool Individual Growth and Development Indicators and the Phonological Awareness and Literacy Screening–PreK," *Early Education and Development* 24, no. 5 (2013): 671–673, https://doi.org/10.1080 /10409289.2012.725620; Janelle J. Montroy et al., "The Texas Kindergarten Entry Assessment: Development, Psychometrics, and Scale-Up of a Comprehensive Screener," *Early Education and Development* 31, no. 5 (2020): 701–734, https://doi.org/10.1080 /10409289.2020.1726700; Georgenne G. Weisenfeld, Karin Garver, and Katherine Hodges, "Federal and State Efforts in the Implementation of Kindergarten Entry Assessments (2011–2018)," *Early Education and Development* 31, no. 5 (2020): 641–647, https://doi.org /10.1080/10409289.2020.1720481.

72. **Mary Walker, born in 1848:** Rita L. Hubbard, *The Oldest Student: How Mary Walker Learned to Read* (New York: Schwartz and Wade Books), 2020.

72. **Walker's dream of literacy:** Hubbard, *The Oldest Student.*

73. **"She studied the alphabet":** Hubbard, *The Oldest Student.*

73. **the better their reading comprehension in third grade:** Monique Sénéchal, Gene Ouellette, and Donna Rodney, "The Misunderstood Giant: On the Predictive Role of Early Vocabulary to Future Reading," in *Handbook of Early Literacy Research*, vol. 2, eds. David K. Dickinson and Susan B. Neuman (New York: Guilford Press, 2006), 174–178.

73. **the better their high school graduation rates:** Donald J. Hernandez, *Double Jeopardy: How Third Grade Reading Skills and Poverty Influence High School Graduation* (Baltimore: The Annie E. Casey Foundation, January 2012), 4–7, https://www.aecf.org/resources/double-jeopardy.

73. **40 "conversational turns" per hour:** LENA Foundation, *Inside Early Talk* (Boulder, CO: LENA, March 2021), 3–4, https://info.lena.org/inside-early-talk.

73. **"talk pedometer":** LENA Foundation, *Inside Early Talk,* 2.

73. **less than they think they do:** Jeffrey A. Richards et al., "How Much Do Parents Think They Talk to Their Child?," *Journal of Early Intervention* 39, no. 3 (September 1, 2017): 166–172, https://doi.org/10.1177/1053815117714567.

74. **"ability to recognize, discriminate, and manipulate the sounds":** Jason L. Anthony and David J. Francis, "Development of Phonological Awareness," *Current Directions in Psychological Science* 14, no. 5 (2005): 255–256, https://doi.org/10.1111/j.0963-7214.2005.00376.x.

74. **a range of skills at different levels:** Anthony and Francis, "Development of Phonological Awareness," 256–257.

75. **related to early growth in word reading skills:** Monica Melby-Lervåg, Solveig-Alma Halaas Lyster, and Charles Hulme, "Phonological Skills and Their Role in Learning to Read: A Meta-Analytic Review," *Psychological Bulletin* 138, no. 2 (2012): 327–330, 338–340, https://doi.org/10.1037/a0026744.

76. **a causal relationship:** Shayne B. Piasta et al., "Increasing Young Children's Contact with Print During Shared Reading: Longitudinal Effects on Literacy Achievement," *Child Development* 83, no. 3 (May/June 2012): 811–818, https://doi.org/10.1111/j.1467-8624.2012.01754.x.

77. **teaching some elements of print in isolation:** Theresa A. Roberts, Patricia F. Vadasy, and Elizabeth A. Sanders, "Preschool Instruction in Letter Names and Sounds: Does Contextualized or Decontextualized Instruction Matter?," *Reading Research Quarterly* 55, no. 4 (October/November/December 2020): 577–595, https://doi.org/10.1002/rrq.284.

77. **distinguish letters from pictures:** Sarah Robins et al., "Parent–Child Conversations about Letters and Pictures," *Reading and Writing* 25 (2012): 2040, https://doi.org/10.1007/s11145-011-9344-5.

78. **predicts letter knowledge in kindergarten:** Tomohiro Inoue et al., "Examining an Extended Home Literacy Model: The Mediating Roles of Emergent Literacy Skills and Reading Fluency," *Scientific Studies of Reading* 22, no. 4, (2018): 274–284, https://doi.org/10.1080/10888438.2018.1435663.

78. **comprehensive reviews:** National Reading Panel (US), *Teaching Children to Read: An Evidence-Based Assessment of the Scientific Research Literature on Reading and Its Implications for Reading Instruction: Reports of the Subgroups* (Bethesda, MD: National Institute of Child Health and Human Development, 2000), 1-1–1-5, 2-1–2-176, https://www.nichd.nih.gov/sites/default/files/publications/pubs/nrp/Documents/report.pdf; Jim Rose, *Independent Review of the Teaching of Early Reading: Final Report* (Nottingham, UK: Department for Education and Skills Publications, 2006), 8, 15–28, https://dera.ioe.ac.uk/5551/2/report.pdf; *National Inquiry into the Teaching of Literacy* (Australia), Australian Government Department of Education, Science, and Training, *Teaching Reading: Report and Recommendations* (Canberra, Australia: Department of Education, Science, and Training, 2005), 31–38, https://research.acer.edu.au/tll_misc/5.

79. **"necessary and nonnegotiable":** Anne Castles, Kathleen Rastle, and Kate Nation, "Ending the Reading Wars: Reading Acquisition from Novice to Expert," *Psychological Science in the Public Interest* 19, no. 1 (2018): 6, https://doi.org/10.1177/1529100618772271.

81. **insight into their understanding:** Gene Ouellette and Monique Sénéchal, "Invented Spelling in Kindergarten as a Predictor of Reading and Spelling in Grade 1: A New Pathway to Literacy, or Just the Same Road, Less Known?," *Developmental Psychology* 53, no. 1 (2017): 79–86, https://doi.org/10.1037/dev0000179.

81. **"detailed study of the letters":** Castles, Rastle, and Nation, "Ending the Reading Wars," 15.

5. NOURISHING WORDS: THE LASTING IMPACT OF EARLY LANGUAGE

83. **an unusual report:** Elizabeth Schaughency et al., "Developing a Community-Based Oral Language Preventive Intervention: Exploring Feasibility and Social Validity for Families Affected by the Canterbury Earthquakes," *Infants and Young Children* 33, no. 3 (September 2020): 195–215, https://doi.org/10.1097/IYC.0000000000000171.

83. **Building facades collapsed:** David Alexander, "Earthquake Rattles Christchurch, New Zealand," *New York Times*, September 3, 2010, World sec., https://www.nytimes.com/slideshow/2010/09/03/world/asia/new-zealand-earthquake.html.

83. **killed 185 people:** Charlotte Graham-McLay, "10 Years after Christchurch Quake, a Hush Where 8,000 Homes Once Stood," *New York Times*, February 21, 2021, https://www.nytimes.com/2021/02/21/world/australia/christchurch-new-zealand-quake-red-zone.html.

84. **performed worse on letter-word identification:** Celia J. Gomez and Hirokazu Yoshikawa, "Earthquake Effects: Estimating the Relationship between Exposure to the 2010 Chilean Earthquake and Preschool Children's Early Cognitive and Executive Function Skills," *Early Childhood Research Quarterly* 38 (1st Quarter 2017): 127–136, https://doi.org/10.1016/j.ecresq.2016.08.004.

84. **struggled with expressive language:** Gail Gillon et al., "A Better Start to Literacy Learning: Findings from a Teacher-Implemented Intervention in Children's First Year at School," *Reading and Writing* 32, no. 8 (October 2019): 1994–1995, https://doi.org/10.1007/s11145-018-9933-7.

84. **"potential developmental sequelae for children":** Schaughency et al., "Developing a Community-Based Oral Language Preventive Intervention," 196.

85. **many well-educated and advantaged families struggle with talk too:** Meredith L. Rowe, "Understanding Socioeconomic Differences in Parents' Speech to Children," *Child Development Perspectives* 12, no. 2 (June 2018): 122–125, https://doi.org/10.1111/cdep.12271.

85. **differences in healthcare outcomes:** Roberta Michnick Golinkoff et al., "Language Matters: Denying the Existence of the 30-Million-Word Gap Has Serious Consequences," *Child Development* 90, no. 3 (May/June 2019): 985–990, https://doi.org/10.1111/cdev.13128.

85. **"Language is causally implicated":** Golinkoff et al., "Language Matters," 986.

85. **"no matter how accurately":** Anne E. Cunningham and Jamie Zibulsky, *Book Smart: How to Develop and Support Successful, Motivated Readers* (New York: Oxford University Press, 2014), 14–15.

86. **"the single strongest action you can take to increase your child's educational opportunities":** Lauren Head Zauche et al., "The Power of Language Nutrition for Children's Brain Development, Health, and Future Academic Achievement," *Journal of Pediatric Health Care* 31, no. 4 (July 2017): 500, https://doi.org/10.1016/j.pedhc.2017.01.007.

86. **35 weeks gestation:** B. S. Kisilevsky et al., "Fetal Sensitivity to Properties of Maternal Speech and Language," *Infant Behavior and Development* 32, no. 1 (January 2009): 59–68, https://doi.org/10.1016/j.infbeh.2008.10.002; Jack P. Shonkoff and Deborah A. Phillips, eds., *From Neurons to Neighborhoods: The Science of Early Childhood Development* (Washington, DC: National Academies Press, 2000), 187–190, https://doi.org/10.17226/9824.

86. **early-language environment predicts:** David K. Dickinson and Michelle V. Porche, "Relation between Language Experiences in Preschool Classrooms and Children's Kindergarten and Fourth-Grade Language and Reading Abilities," *Child Development* 82, no. 3 (May/June 2011): 872–881, https://doi.org/10.1111/j.1467-8624.2011.01576.x.

87. **statewide campaign called Talk With Me Baby:** Susan Brasher et al., "Integrating Early Brain Science and Skills into Prelicensure Nursing Curriculum to Promote Parent-Child Interaction," *Nurse Educator* 46, no. 4 (July/August 2021): E75–E77, https://doi.org/10.1097/NNE.0000000000000983.

88. **In the *I Do* step:** "NURSES," Talk With Me Baby, https://www.talkwithmebaby.org/nurses.

88. **Brains differ at birth:** Usha C. Goswami, *Child Psychology: A Very Short Introduction* (New York: Oxford University Press, 2014), 6; Hakon Jonsson et al., "Differences between Germline Genomes of Monozygotic Twins," *Nature Genetics* 53, no. 1 (2021): 27–33, https://doi.org/10.1038/s41588-020-00755-1.

88. **it's their environment that makes these differences trivial or meaningful:** Goswami, *Child Psychology*, 6.

89. **Child-directed speech supports language learning:** Golinkoff et al., "Language Matters," 987–988.

90. **infants prefer listening to this "baby talk":** Jessica F. Schwab and Casey Lew-Williams, "Language Learning, Socioeconomic Status, and Child-Directed Speech," *WIREs Cognitive Science* 7, no. 4 (July/August 2016): 265–269, https://doi.org/10.1002/wcs.1393.

90. **they match what they observe:** Margaret Addabbo et al., "'Something in the Way You Move': Infants Are Sensitive to Emotions Conveyed in Action Kinematics," *Developmental Science* 23, no. 1 (2020): e12873, https://doi.org/10.1111/desc.12873.

90. **give your child the richest vocabulary, most fluent speech, and deepest background knowledge:** Ellen Bialystok, "Second-Language Acquisition and Bilingualism at an Early Age and the Impact on Early Cognitive Development," in R. E. Tremblay, R. G. Barr, and R. D. Peters, eds., *Encyclopedia on Early Childhood Development* (Montreal: Centre of Excellence for Early Childhood Development, updated September 2017), 1–5, https://www.child-encyclopedia.com/pdf/expert/second-language/according-experts/second-language-acquisition-and-bilingualism-early-age-and-impact.

90. **help toddlers grasp common nouns:** Thea Cameron-Faulkner, Elena Lieven, and Michael Tomasello, "A Construction Based Analysis of Child Directed Speech," *Cognitive Science* 27, no. 6 (November 2003): 848–870, https://doi.org/10.1016/j.cogsci.2003.06.001.

90. **body movements capture infant attention:** Catherine S. Tamis-LeMonda, Yana Kuchirko, and Lulu Song, "Why Is Infant Language Learning Facilitated by Parental Responsiveness?," *Current Directions in Psychological Science* 23, no. 2 (2014): 123–124, https://doi.org/10.1177/0963721414522813.

91. **predictive of kids' language achievements:** Pamela Nicely, Catherine S. Tamis-LeMonda, and Marc H. Bornstein, "Mothers' Attuned Responses to Infant Affect Expressivity Promote Earlier Achievement of Language Milestones," *Infant Behavior and Development* 22, no. 4 (1999): 557–566, https://doi.org/10.1016/S0163-6383(00)00023-0.

91. **by 11 months:** Ed Donnellan et al., "Infants' Intentionally Communicative Vocalizations Elicit Responses from Caregivers and Are the Best Predictors of the Transition to Language: A Longitudinal Investigation of Infants' Vocalizations, Gestures and Word Production," *Developmental Science* 23, no. 1 (January 2020): e12843, https://doi.org/10.1111/desc.12843.

91. **1.4 million more words:** Jessica Logan et al., "When Children Are Not Read to at Home: The Million Word Gap," *Journal of Developmental and Behavioral Pediatrics* 40, no. 5 (June 2019): 384–385, https://doi.org/10.1097/DBP.0000000000000657.

92. **more novel, challenging, and enriching:** Dominic W. Massaro, "Two Different Communication Genres and Implications for Vocabulary Development and Learning to

Read," *Journal of Literacy Research* 47, no. 4 (2015): 507–521, https://doi.org/10.1177/1086296X15627528.

92. **a style of reading aloud that fosters comment and discussion:** Schaughency et al., "Developing a Community-Based Oral Language Preventive Intervention," 195–218.

93. **"Part of mindfulness is":** *Ten Percent Happier Meditation*, iPhone app, v. 6.4.0 (10% Happier Inc., 2021); Joseph Goldstein, Essential Advice course, "Session 14: More Than a Hobby."

94. **Tuning in to your baby:** Carolyn Brockmeyer Cates et al., "Leveraging Healthcare to Promote Responsive Parenting: Impacts of the Video Interaction Project on Parenting Stress," *Journal of Child and Family Studies* 25, no. 3 (March 2016): 827–834, https://doi.org/10.1007/s10826-015-0267-7.

94. **coping mechanisms:** Cates et al., "Leveraging Healthcare," 829–833; Per Ivar Kaaresen et al., "A Randomized, Controlled Trial of the Effectiveness of an Early-Intervention Program in Reducing Parenting Stress after Preterm Birth," *Pediatrics* 118, no. 1 (July 2006): e10–e16, https://doi.org/10.1542/peds.2005-1491; Deborah Gross, Louis Fogg, and Sharon Tucker, "The Efficacy of Parent Training for Promoting Positive Parent–Toddler Relationships," *Research in Nursing and Health* 18, no. 6 (December 1995): 490–498, https://doi.org/10.1002/nur.4770180605; Sharon Telleen, Allen Herzog, and Teresa Kilbane, "Impact of a Family Support Program on Mothers' Social Support and Parenting Stress," *American Journal of Orthopsychiatry* 59, no. 3 (July 1989): 410–418, https://doi.org/10.1111/j.1939-0025.1989.tb01676.x.

94. **a steep incline:** Keith A. Crnic and Cathryn L. Booth, "Mothers' and Fathers' Perceptions of Daily Hassles of Parenting across Early Childhood," *Journal of Marriage and Family* 53, no. 4 (November 1991): 1043–1045, https://doi.org/10.2307/353007; Marion O'Brien, "Child-Rearing Difficulties Reported by Parents of Infants and Toddlers," *Journal of Pediatric Psychology* 21, no. 3 (June 1996): 435–441, https://doi.org/10.1093/jpepsy/21.3.433.

95. **Routine parenting work:** John Taylor, "Structural Validity of the Parenting Daily Hassles Intensity Scale," *Stress and Health* 35, no. 2 (April 2019): 176–185, https://doi.org/10.1002/smi.2852.

97. **predicted language skills 8 months later:** Amber Muhinyi and Meredith L. Rowe, "Shared Reading with Preverbal Infants and Later Language Development," *Journal of Applied Developmental Psychology* 64 (July 1, 2019): 101053, https://doi.org/10.1016/j.appdev.2019.101053.

6. TAKING TURNS: HOW TO MAKE CONVERSATION A HABIT FROM DAY ONE

100. **enormous differences:** Meredith L. Rowe, "Understanding Socioeconomic Differences in Parents' Speech to Children," *Child Development Perspectives* 12, no. 2 (June 2018): 122–125, https://doi.org/10.1111/cdep.12271; Janellen Huttenlocher et al., "Sources of Variability in Children's Language Growth," *Cognitive Psychology* 61, no. 4 (December 1, 2010): 343–363, https://doi.org/10.1016/j.cogpsych.2010.08.002; Mary E. Brushe et al., "How Many Words Are Australian Children Hearing in the First Year of Life?," *BMC Pediatrics* 20, article no. 52 (February 3, 2020): 2–8, https://doi.org/10.1186/s12887-020-1946-0.

100. **Parent talkativeness varies:** Rowe, "Understanding Socioeconomic Differences," 123–124; Catherine S. Tamis-LeMonda, Yana Kuchirko, and Lulu Song, "Why Is Infant Language Learning Facilitated by Parental Responsiveness?," *Current Directions in Psychological Science* 23, no. 2 (April 1, 2014): 122–125, https://doi.org/10.1177/0963721414522813.

100. **talkative parents have talkative little ones:** Jill Gilkerson and Jeffrey A. Richards, *The Power of Talk, 2nd ed.: Impact of Adult Talk, Conversational Turns, and TV During the Critical 0–4 Years of Child Development*. LENA Foundation Technical Report LTR-01-2 (Boulder, CO: LENA Foundation, 2009), 18.

100. **learning outcomes years later:** Lauren Head Zauche et al., "The Power of Language Nutrition for Children's Brain Development, Health, and Future Academic Achievement," *Journal of Pediatric Health Care* 31, no. 4 (July 2017): 500, https://doi .org/10.1016/j.pedhc.2017.01.007; David K. Dickinson and Michelle V. Porche, "Relation Between Language Experiences in Preschool Classrooms and Children's Kindergarten and Fourth-Grade Language and Reading Abilities," *Child Development* 82, no. 3 (May/June 2011): 872–881, https://doi.org/10.1111/j.1467 -8624.2011.01576.x.

101. **overestimate how much we talk:** Jeffrey A. Richards et al., "How Much Do Parents Think They Talk to Their Child?," *Journal of Early Intervention* 39, no. 3 (September 1, 2017): 166–172, https://doi.org/10.1177/1053815117714567.

101. **40 conversational turns:** LENA, *Inside Early Talk* (Boulder, CO: LENA Foundation, March 2021), 3–4, https://info.lena.org/inside-early-talk.

102. **higher IQs in middle school:** Jill Gilkerson et al., "Language Experience in the Second Year of Life and Language Outcomes in Late Childhood," *Pediatrics* 142, no. 4 (October 2018): 2–7, https://doi.org/10.1542/peds.2017-4276.

102. **transcribed and coded the data by hand:** Betty Hart and Todd R. Risley, *Meaningful Differences in the Everyday Experience of Young American Children* (Baltimore: Brookes, 1995), 21–48.

103. **separates talk from other vocalizations:** LENA, "LENA Pro," https://shop.lena.org /products/lena-pro; LENA, "Understanding LENA Technology," https://www.lena.org /technology.

103. **More than 10,000 children:** Steven M. Hannon, "Making a Difference: We Reached Our Goal to Impact 10,000 Children in 2019!," LENA, December 10, 2019, https://www.lena.org/year-in-review-2019.

103. **peaks and valleys of talk:** LENA, *Inside Early Talk*, 6–7.

105. **Fogg recommends:** B. J. Fogg, *Tiny Habits: The Small Changes That Change Everything*, First Mariner Books ed. (Boston: Houghton Mifflin Harcourt, 2020), 6.

109. **Like so many of us:** Richards et al., "How Much Do Parents Think They Talk to Their Child?," 166–172.

110. **doubled from 1.32 hours:** Weiwei Chen and Jessica L. Adler, "Assessment of Screen Exposure in Young Children, 1997 to 2014," *JAMA Pediatrics* 173, no. 4 (April 1, 2019): 391–392, https://doi.org/10.1001/jamapediatrics.2018.5546.

110. **toddlers struggle to learn from video:** Gabrielle A. Strouse et al., "Co-Viewing Supports Toddlers' Word Learning from Contingent and Noncontingent Video," *Journal of Experimental Child Psychology* 166 (February 1, 2018): 313–322, https://doi.org/10.1016/j.jecp.2017.09.005.

110. **negative correlation between hours of television:** Gilkerson and Richards, *The Power of Talk*, 16.

111. **worse performance on developmental screenings:** Sheri Madigan et al., "Association between Screen Time and Children's Performance on a Developmental Screening Test," *JAMA Pediatrics* 173, no. 3 (March 1, 2019): 245–248, https://doi.org /10.1001/jamapediatrics.2018.5056.

111. **"co-view, talk, and teach":** "Healthy Digital Media Use Habits for Babies, Toddlers & Preschoolers," HealthyChildren.org, November 12, 2019, https://www .healthychildren.org/English/family-life/Media/Pages/Healthy-Digital-Media-Use -Habits-for-Babies-Toddlers-Preschoolers.aspx.

111. *4 hours per day* **exposed to screens:** Pooja S. Tandon et al., "Preschoolers' Total Daily Screen Time at Home and by Type of Child Care," *Journal of Pediatrics* 158, no. 2 (February 1, 2011): 297–298, https://doi.org/10.1016/j.jpeds.2010.08.005.

111. **four times the American Academy of Pediatrics' recommendation:** "Where We Stand: Screen Time," HealthyChildren.org, November 1, 2016, https://www
.healthychildren.org/English/family-life/Media/Pages/Where-We-Stand-TV-Viewing
-Time.aspx.

111. **valuable alphabetic knowledge:** Shalom M. Fisch, Rosemarie T. Truglio, and Charlotte F. Cole, "The Impact of Sesame Street on Preschool Children: A Review and Synthesis of 30 Years' Research," *Media Psychology* 1, no. 2 (1999): 167–171, https://doi.org/10.1207
/s1532785xmep0102_5; Deborah L. Linebarger, "Super Why! to the Rescue: Can Preschoolers Learn Early Literacy Skills from Educational Television?," *International Journal for Cross-Disciplinary Subjects in Education* 6, no. 1 (March 2015): 2060–2063, https://doi.org/10.20533/ijcdse.2042.6364.2015.0286.

112. **"increase the burden for parents in later life":** Jin Zhao et al., "Excessive Screen Time and Psychosocial Well-Being: The Mediating Role of Body Mass Index, Sleep Duration, and Parent-Child Interaction," *The Journal of Pediatrics* 202 (November 2018): 161, https://
doi.org/10.1016/j.jpeds.2018.06.029.

112. **screen-time exposure is associated with kids' increased risk:** Zhao et al., "Excessive Screen Time," 157–160.

112. **Thousands of families have signed on:** "Screen-Free Saturdays," Fairplay, https://www
.screenfree.org/saturdays.

112. **less engaged with and responsive to kids:** Brooke Auxier et al., *Parenting Children in the Age of Screens* (Washington, DC: Pew Research Center, July 2020), 11–12, 47–49, 53–55, https://www.pewresearch.org/internet/wp-content/uploads/sites/9/2020/07/PI_2020.07
.28_kids-and-screens_FINAL.pdf; Jenny Radesky et al., "Maternal Mobile Device Use During a Structured Parent–Child Interaction Task," *Academic Pediatrics* 15, no. 2 (March 2015): 239–242, https://doi.org/10.1016/j.acap.2014.10.001; Cory A. Kildare and Wendy Middlemiss, "Impact of Parents Mobile Device Use on Parent-Child Interaction: A Literature Review," *Computers in Human Behavior* 75 (October 1, 2017): 579–591, https://doi.org/10.1016/J.chb.2017.06.003.

113. **A survey of 2,000 parents:** "When It Comes to Screen Time, Parents Are Just as Guilty as Their Children," PR Newswire, October 21, 2019, https://www.prnewswire.com/news
-releases/when-it-comes-to-screen-time-parents-are-just-as-guilty-as-their-children-300
941553.html.

113. **"paying attention in a particular way":** Jon Kabat-Zinn, *Wherever You Go There You Are: Mindfulness Meditation in Everyday Life* (New York: Hachette Go, 2020), 4.

113. **reduce caregiver stress and coparenting disagreements:** Virginia Burgdorf, Marianna Szabó, and Maree J. Abbott, "The Effect of Mindfulness Interventions for Parents on Parenting Stress and Youth Psychological Outcomes: A Systematic Review and Meta-Analysis," *Frontiers in Psychology* 10, no. 1336 (June 6, 2019): 3–19, https://doi.org
/10.3389/fpsyg.2019.01336; Susan M. Bögels, Annukka Lehtonen, and Kathleen Restifo, "Mindful Parenting in Mental Health Care," *Mindfulness* 1 (May 2010): 115–17, https://doi.org/10.1007/s12671-010-0014-5.

114. **reduction in the students' cravings for their smartphones:** Yukun Lan et al., "A Pilot Study of a Group Mindfulness-Based Cognitive-Behavioral Intervention for Smartphone Addiction among University Students," *Journal of Behavioral Addictions* 7, no. 4 (November 2018): 1172–1175, https://doi.org/10.1556/2006.7.2018.103.

114. **"created room for more conscious decision-making":** Marta Brzosko, "How to Overcome Your Phone Addiction with Mindfulness," *Better Humans*, January 28, 2020, https://
betterhumans.pub/how-to-overcome-your-phone-addiction-with-mindfulness-a48e
2eae72ef.

114. **sit with our devices in hand:** Mitch Abblett, "Addicted to Your Phone? Try This Practice—Phone in Hand," *Mindful* (blog), March 14, 2016, https://www.mindful.org /addicted-to-your-phone-try-this-practice-phone-in-hand.

114. **"We simply (and yet with great difficulty)":** Abblett, "Addicted to Your Phone?"

115. **recommends celebrating your habit three times:** Fogg, *Tiny Habits,* 151–152.

115. **"Emotions create habits":** Fogg, *Tiny Habits,* 137.

116. **feel-good hormone oxytocin:** Gabriela Markova, "The Games Infants Play: Social Games during Early Mother–Infant Interactions and Their Relationship with Oxytocin," *Frontiers in Psychology* 9, no. 1041 (June 25, 2018): 2–7, https://doi.org/10.3389 /fpsyg.2018.01041.

7. SOUND INSTRUCTION: THE TENOR OF READING SUCCESS

119. **Archival footage:** "Shirley Ellis 'The Name Game' (Merv Griffin Show 1965)," accessed January 3, 2022, Dailymotion video, 5:04, https://www.dailymotion.com/video/x2xxzqn; "'The Name Game' by Shirley Ellis," accessed January 3, 2022, YouTube video, 3:03, https://www.youtube.com/watch?v=LulWZQo46Ao.

119. **music history footnote:** "Hot Rhythm and Blues Singles," *Billboard (Archive: 1963–2000)* 77, no. 5 (January 30, 1965): 14, Entertainment Industry Magazine Archive; Malcolm Baumgart and Mick Patrick, "The Name of the Game: The Story of Shirley Ellis," Spectropop, accessed January 3, 2022, http://www.spectropop.com/ShirleyEllis.

119. **Runway models walked:** Barry Janoff, "When Shopping at Kmart Can Be a 'Hazzard,'" *Brandweek,* May 8, 2006, 44; "Defining Moments," *WWD: Women's Wear Daily* 19, no. 69 (Fall 2006): 36–42.

120. **his "schtick with kids":** "'The Name Game' Is Howard's Secret Weapon with Children," May 3, 2017, https://www.howardstern.com/show/2017/05/03/name-game-howards-secret -weapon-children.

120. **trade articles:** Mark Holgate, "The Name Game," *Vogue* (July 2011), 68; Bernie Pacyniak, "The Name Game," *Candy Industry* (February 2004), 8.

120. **encyclopedia entry documenting "proto-rap":** Eddie Bonilla, "Proto-Rap," in *St. James Encyclopedia of Hip Hop Culture,* ed. Thomas J. Riggs (Farmington Hills, MI: St. James Press, 2018).

120. **nitty-gritty:** "The Nitty Gritty" was Ellis's first big hit, released by Congress Recordings in 1963. Phil Hardy, "Shirley Ellis," in *The Faber Companion to 20th Century Popular Music* (London: Faber and Faber, 2001).

121. **knowledge of certain units develops and consolidates faster than others:** Jason L. Anthony and David J. Francis, "Development of Phonological Awareness," *Current Directions in Psychological Science* 14, no. 5 (2005): 255–258, https://doi.org/10.1111/j.0963 -7214.2005.00376.x.

125. **"Auditory imagery":** Timothy L. Hubbard, "Auditory Imagery: Empirical Findings," *Psychological Bulletin* 136, no. 2 (March 2010): 310–311, 320–321, https://doi.org/10.1037 /a0018436.

125. **pictures of the mouth positions:** Nancy Boyer and Linnea C. Ehri, "Contribution of Phonemic Segmentation Instruction with Letters and Articulation Pictures to Word Reading and Spelling in Beginners," *Scientific Studies of Reading* 15, no. 5 (2011): 443–461, https://doi.org/10.1080/10888438.2010.520778; Linnea C. Ehri, "The Science of Learning to Read Words: A Case for Systematic Phonics Instruction," *Reading Research Quarterly* 55, no. S1 (August 2020): S53, https://doi.org/10.1002/rrq.334.

126. **whose shape includes the target letter:** Linnea C. Ehri, Nancy D. Deffner, and Lee S. Wilce, "Pictorial Mnemonics for Phonics," *Journal of Educational Psychology* 76, no. 5 (October 1984): 882–891, https://doi.org/10.1037/0022-0663.76.5.880.

127. **transfers to phonological awareness and improves word-reading skills in English:** Jason L. Anthony et al., "Development of Bilingual Phonological Awareness in Spanish-Speaking English Language Learners: The Roles of Vocabulary, Letter Knowledge, and Prior Phonological Awareness," *Scientific Studies of Reading* 13, no. 6 (November 9, 2009): 537–555, https://doi.org/10.1080/10888430903034770; Aydin Y. Durgunoğlu, William E. Nagy, and Barbara J. Hancin-Bhatt, "Cross-Language Transfer of Phonological Awareness," *Journal of Educational Psychology* 85, no. 3 (September 1993): 454–462, https://doi.org /10.1037/0022-0663.85.3.453.

128. **cross-language transfer:** Brenda A. Wawire and Young-Suk G. Kim, "Cross-Language Transfer of Phonological Awareness and Letter Knowledge: Causal Evidence and Nature of Transfer," *Scientific Studies of Reading* 22, no. 6 (June 6, 2018): 446–455, https://doi.org /10.1080/10888438.2018.1474882; Hedi Kwakkel et al., "The Impact of Lexical Skills and Executive Functioning on L1 and L2 Phonological Awareness in Bilingual Kindergarten," *Learning and Individual Differences* 88 (May 1, 2021): 102009, 2–7, https://doi.org/10.1016 /j.lindif.2021.102009; Anthony et al., "Development of Bilingual Phonological Awareness," 537–555; Durgunoğlu, Nagy, and Hancin-Bhatt, "Cross-Language Transfer," 454–462.

128. **heavily influenced by oral-language ability:** Elinor Saiegh-Haddad, "What Is Phonological Awareness in L2?," *Journal of Neurolinguistics*, 50 (May 1, 2019): 17–25, https://doi.org/10.1016/j.jneuroling.2017.11.001.

129. **"How can I teach reading":** Marcelle Haddix, *Cultivating Racial and Linguistic Diversity in Literacy Teacher Education: Teachers Like Me* (New York: Routledge, 2016), https:// doi.org/10.4324/9781315850665.

130. **is spoken by the majority of black elementary schoolers in the United States:** Barbara Zurer Pearson, Tracy Conner, and Janice E. Jackson, "Removing Obstacles for African American English-Speaking Children through Greater Understanding of Language Difference," *Developmental Psychology*, 49, no. 1 (January 2013): 31–44, https://doi.org /10.1037/a0028248.

130. **spell *ticket* as *tickit* at higher rates:** Rebecca Treiman and Margo Bowman, "Spelling in African American Children: The Case of Final Consonant Devoicing," *Reading and Writing* 28, (March 2015): 1014, https://doi.org/10.1007/s11145-015-9559-y.

131. **a handbook of linguistics:** Michael Hammond, "Prosodic Phonology," in *The Handbook of English Linguistics*, eds. April McMahon and Bas Aarts (Malden, MA: John Wiley & Sons, Incorporated, 2006), 421–422.

8: L IS FOR LIBERATION: HOW TO HELP KIDS CRACK THE ALPHABETIC CODE

134. **"should know nothing but to obey his master":** Frederick Douglass, *Narrative of the Life of Frederick Douglass* (Oxford: Oxford University Press, 1999), 39, EBSCO Publishing eBook Collection.

134. **down to the first joint:** Janet Cornelius, "'We Slipped and Learned to Read': Slave Accounts of the Literacy Process, 1830–1865," *Phylon (1960–)* 44, no. 3 (1983): 174, https://doi.org/10.2307/274930.

134. **stiffer and stiffer anti-literacy statutes:** Heather Andrea Williams, *Self-Taught: African American Education in Slavery and Freedom* (Chapel Hill: University of North Carolina Press, 2005), 205, 207–208.

134. **"Reading indicated to the world":** Williams, *Self-Taught*, 7.

134. **"the pathway from slavery to freedom":** Douglass, *Narrative of the Life*, 39.

134. **He mastered the letters:** Douglass, *Narrative of the Life*, 43, 46–47; David W. Blight, *Frederick Douglass: Prophet of Freedom* (New York: Simon & Schuster, 2018), 42.

135. **5 percent succeeded:** James D. Anderson, *The Education of Blacks in the South, 1860–1935* (Chapel Hill: University of North Carolina Press, 1988), 16.

135. **"language of instruction":** Laura S. Tortorelli, Ryan P. Bowles, and Lori E. Skibbe, "Easy as AcHGzrjq: The Quick Letter Name Knowledge Assessment," *Reading Teacher* 71, no. 2 (September/October 2017): 146, https://doi.org/10.1002/trtr.1608.

135. **substantially fewer letter names:** Ryan P. Bowles et al., "Item Response Analysis of Uppercase and Lowercase Letter Name Knowledge," *Journal of Psychoeducational Assessment* 32, no. 2 (April 2014): 148–149, https://doi.org/10.1177/0734282913490266; Tara M. Strang and Shayne B. Piasta, "Socioeconomic Differences in Code-Focused Emergent Literacy Skills," *Reading and Writing* 29, no. 7 (September 2016): 1348, 1353–1354, https://doi.org/10.1007/s11145-016-9639-7.

136. **likely to hear phrases:** Tortorelli, Bowles, and Skibbe, "Easy as AcHGzrjq," 146.

136. **Letter names give:** Marilyn Jager Adams, *Beginning to Read: Thinking and Learning about Print* (Cambridge, MA: MIT Press, 1994), 351.

136. **a tool for grasping and remembering the sounds:** Rebecca Treiman et al., "The Foundations of Literacy: Learning the Sounds of Letters," *Child Development* 69, no. 6 (December 1998): 1526–1539, https://doi.org/10.2307/1132130; Laura M. Justice et al., "An Investigation of Four Hypotheses Concerning the Order by Which 4-Year-Old Children Learn the Alphabet Letters," *Early Childhood Research Quarterly* 21, no. 3 (2006): 379–384, https://doi.org/10.1016/j.ecresq.2006.07.010; Mary Ann Evans et al., "Letter Names, Letter Sounds and Phonological Awareness: An Examination of Kindergarten Children Across Letters and of Letters Across Children," *Reading and Writing* 19 (2006): 963–984, https://doi.org/10.1007/s11145-006-9026-x.

136. **foretelling later reading achievement:** Donna M. Scanlon and Frank R. Vellutino, "Prerequisite Skills, Early Instruction, and Success in First-Grade Reading: Selected Results from a Longitudinal Study," *Mental Retardation and Developmental Disabilities Research Reviews* 2 (1996): 57–58, https://doi.org/10.1002/(SICI)1098-2779(1996)2:1<54::AID-MRDD9>3.0.CO;2-X.

136. **Preschool, kindergarten, and early-intervention program curricula:** Francis L. Huang, "Does Attending a State-Funded Preschool Program Improve Letter Name Knowledge?," *Early Childhood Research Quarterly* 38 (2017): 117, https://doi.org/10.1016/j.ecresq.2016.08.002.

137. **significantly fewer letter names:** Strang and Piasta, "Socioeconomic Differences," 1348–1355.

137. **large-scale pre-K evaluation:** Huang, "Does Attending a State-Funded Preschool Program Improve Letter Name Knowledge?," 124.

137. **likely to struggle:** Shayne B. Piasta, Yaacov Petscher, and Laura M. Justice, "How Many Letters Should Preschoolers in Public Programs Know? The Diagnostic Efficiency of Various Preschool Letter-Naming Benchmarks for Predicting First-Grade Literacy Achievement," *Journal of Educational Psychology* 104, no. 4 (2012): 950–951, https://doi.org/10.1037/a0027757.

137. **Common Core State Standards:** "English Language Arts Standards >> Reading: Foundational Skills >> Kindergarten >> 1 >> d," Common Core State Standards Initiative, http://www.corestandards.org/ELA-Literacy/RF/K/1/d.

138. **compared with their colleagues in 1998:** Daphna Bassok, Scott Latham, and Anna Rorem, "Is Kindergarten the New First Grade?," *AERA Open* 1, no. 4 (January–March 2016): 5–6, https://doi.org/10.1177/2332858415616358.

138. **"more pronounced":** Bassok, Latham, and Rorem, "Is Kindergarten the New First Grade?," 14.

140. **2D marks to be deciphered:** Sarah Robins et al., "Parent–Child Conversations about Letters and Pictures," *Reading and Writing* 25 (2012): 2040, https://doi.org/10.1007 /s11145-011-9344-5.

140. **In questionnaires:** Felicity Martini and Monique Sénéchal, "Learning Literacy Skills at Home: Parent Teaching, Expectations, and Child Interest," *Canadian Journal of Behavioural Science* 44, no. 3 (2012): 214–217, https://doi.org/10.1037/a0026758.

140. **high expectations:** Martini and Sénéchal, "Learning Literacy Skills at Home," 212–213, 215.

141. **pioneering researcher Marilyn Jager Adams:** Adams, *Beginning to Read*, 351.

141. **labeled buckets:** Adams, *Beginning to Read*, 351.

141. **letter-name knowledge:** Rebecca Treiman and Sloane Wolter, "Use of Letter Names Benefits Young Children's Spelling," *Psychological Science* 31, no. 1 (December 2019): 4–5, https://doi.org/10.1177/0956797619888837.

141. **accelerates letter-sound learning:** Shayne B. Piasta and Richard K. Wagner, "Learning Letter Names and Sounds: Effects of Instruction, Letter Type, and Phonological Processing Skill," *Journal of Experimental Child Psychology* 105 (2010): 339, https://doi.org/10.1016/j .jecp.2009.12.008.

142. **Analyses of parent-child conversations:** Rebecca Treiman et al., "Parents' Talk about Letters with Their Young Children," *Child Development* 86, no. 5 (September/October 2015): 1415–1416, https://doi.org/10.1111/cdev.12385.

143. **breaks and junctures within them:** Anna C. Both-de Vries and Adriana G. Bus, "Visual Processing of Pictures and Letters in Alphabet Books and the Implications for Letter Learning," *Contemporary Educational Psychology* 39, no. 2 (April 2014): 160–162, https://doi.org/10.1016/j.cedpsych.2014.03.005.

144. **from A to Z:** Cindy D. Jones and D. Ray Reutzel, "Enhanced Alphabet Knowledge Instruction: Exploring a Change of Frequency, Focus, and Distributed Cycles of Review," *Reading Psychology* 33, no. 5 (2012): 449, https://doi.org/10.1080/02702711.2010.545260.

145. **are among the easiest to name and write:** Shayne B. Piasta, "Moving to Assessment-Guided Differentiated Instruction to Support Young Children's Alphabet Knowledge," *Reading Teacher* 68, no. 3 (November 2014): 206, https://doi.org/10.1002/trtr.1316; Beth M. Phillips et al., "IRTs of the ABCs: Children's Letter Name Acquisition," *Journal of School Psychology* 50, no. 4 (August 2012): 468–474, https://doi.org/10.1016/ j.jsp.2012.05.002; Laura M. Justice et al., "An Investigation of Four Hypotheses Concerning the Order by Which 4-Year-Old Children Learn the Alphabet Letters," *Early Childhood Research Quarterly* 21 (2006), 381; Cynthia Puranik, Yaacov Petscher, and Christopher Lonigan, "Dimensionality and Reliability of Letter Writing in 3-to 5-Year-Old Preschool Children," *Learning and Individual Differences* 28 (2013): 138–139.

145. **stronger readers at the end of kindergarten:** Treiman et al., "Parents' Talk about Letters with Their Young Children," 1411–1412.

145. **wide array of early-childhood programs:** Phillips et al., "IRTs of the ABCs."

145. **a "typical order":** Piasta, "Moving to Assessment-Guided Differentiated Instruction," 206.

146. **faster pace of letter instruction:** Kristin Sunde, Bjarte Furnes, and Kjersti Lundetræ, "Does Introducing the Letters Faster Boost the Development of Children's Letter Knowledge, Word Reading and Spelling in the First Year of School?," *Scientific Studies of Reading* 24, no. 2 (March 3, 2020): 142–155, https://doi.org/10.1080/10888 438.2019.1615491.

147. **Researchers estimate:** Both-de Vries and Bus, "Visual Processing of Pictures and Letters," 160.

147. **"That might seem somehow limiting":** Perry Nodelman, "A Is for . . . What? The Function of Alphabet Books," *Journal of Early Childhood Literacy* 1, no. 3 (2001): 247, https://doi.org/10.1177/14687984010013001.

148. **embedded in the signs and labels:** Michelle M. Neumann, "The Effects of a Parent–Child Environmental Print Program on Emergent Literacy," *Journal of Early Childhood Research* 16, no. 4 (December 2018): 338, https://doi.org/10.1177/1476718X18809120.

148. **The strategies encompassed:** Neumann, "The Effects of a Parent–Child Environmental Print Program," 339–343.

9. WORD WISDOM: HOW TO SPELL YOUR WAY TO BETTER READING

153. **first black student to make it to the final round:** Maria Cramer and Alexandra E. Petri, "Behind Zaila Avant-garde's Win, a History of Struggle for Black Spellers," *New York Times*, July 11, 2021, U.S. sec., https://www.nytimes.com/2021/07/11/us/spelling-bee -racism-zaila-avant-garde.html.

153. **excavated Cox's incredible story:** Michael Romain, "The Tragedy of MacNolia Cox," May 20, 2015, *Wednesday Journal of Oak Park and River Forest*, May 20, 2015, https://www .oakpark.com/2015/05/20/the-tragedy-of-macnolia-cox.

154. **ride in segregated train cars:** April White, "Spelling Bee Champ Zaila Avant-garde Was Inspired by a Black Girl Named MacNolia Cox. This Is Why," *Washington Post*, July 10, 2021, https://www.washingtonpost.com/history/2021/07/10/macnolia-cox-zaila-avant -garde-spelling-bee.

154. **Cox spelled flawlessly:** Romain, "The Tragedy of MacNolia Cox."

154. **a word that wasn't on the approved list:** Cramer and Petri, "Behind Zaila Avant-garde's Win."

154. **died of cancer, a domestic:** White, "Spelling Bee Champ"; Romain, "The Tragedy of MacNolia Cox."

154. **tells Cox's life story in reverse:** A. Van Jordan, *M-A-C-N-O-L-I-A: Poems* (New York: W. W. Norton & Company, 2005), 1–144.

154. **"Historically, African-Americans have understood":** Cynthia R. Greenlee, "The Word Is 'Nemesis': The Fight to Integrate the National Spelling Bee," *Longreads*, June 5, 2017, https://longreads.com/2017/06/05/the-word-is-nemesis-the-fight-to-integrate-the -national-spelling-bee.

155. **Errors in job applications:** Christelle Martin-Lacroux and Alain Lacroux, "Do Employers Forgive Applicants' Bad Spelling in Résumés?," *Business and Professional Communication Quarterly* 80, no. 3 (2017), 323–329, https://doi.org/10.1177/2329490616671310; Christelle Martin-Lacroux, "'Without the Spelling Errors I Would Have Shortlisted Her . . .': The Impact of Spelling Errors on Recruiters' Choice During the Personnel Selection Process," *International Journal of Selection and Assessment* 25, no. 3 (September 2017): 277–281, https://doi.org/10.1111/ijsa.12179.

156. **the faster you'll read the word:** Sandra Martin-Chang, Gene Ouellette, and Melanie Madden, "Does Poor Spelling Equate to Slow Reading? The Relationship Between Reading, Spelling, and Orthographic Quality," *Reading and Writing* 27, no. 8 (2014): 1489–1501, https://doi.org/10.1007/s11145-014-9502-7; Gene Ouellette, Sandra Martin-Chang, and Maya Rossi, "Learning from Our Mistakes: Improvements in Spelling Lead to Gains in Reading Speed," *Scientific Studies of Reading* 21, no. 4 (2017): 351–355, https://doi .org/10.1080/10888438.2017.1306064; Maya Rossi, Sandra Martin-Chang, and Gene Ouellette, "Exploring the Space between Good and Poor Spelling: Orthographic Quality and Reading Speed," *Scientific Studies of Reading* 23, no. 2 (2019): 192–197, https://doi.org /10.1080/10888438.2018.1508213.

156. **directly linked to sight-word reading, reading fluency, and even third-grade reading:** David D. Paige et al., "A Path Analytic Model Linking Foundational Skills to Grade 3 State Reading Achievement," *Journal of Educational Research* (2018): 3–9, https://doi.org/10.1080 /00220671.2018.1445609.

156. **supporting better phonological awareness and reading skills:** Steve Graham and Tanya Santangelo, "Does Spelling Instruction Make Students Better Spellers, Readers, and Writers? A Meta-Analytic Review," *Reading and Writing* 27 (2014): 1706–1736; R. Malatesha Joshi et al., "How Words Cast Their Spell," *American Educator* 32 (Winter 2008–2009): 7–10.

156. **at risk of receiving lower grades in other subjects:** Steve Graham, Karen R. Harris, and Michael Hebert, "It Is More Than Just the Message: Analysis of Presentation Effects in Scoring Writing," *Focus on Exceptional Children* 44, no. 4 (2011): 1–12.

156. **"the abandoned stepchild in the family of language arts":** Joshi et al., "How Words Cast Their Spell," 9.

157. **the vast majority of elementary school teachers say:** Antoinette Doyle, Jing Zhang, and Chris Mattatall, "Spelling Instruction in the Primary Grades: Teachers' Beliefs, Practices, and Concerns," *Reading Horizons* 54, no. 2 (2015): 21, https://scholarworks.wmich.edu /reading_horizons/vol54/iss2/2; Francine R. Johnston, "Exploring Classroom Teachers' Spelling Practices and Beliefs," *Reading Research and Instruction* 40, no. 2 (Winter 2001): 144–47, 150, https://doi.org/10.1080/19388070109558339.

159. **tend to write common letters (e.g., E, T, and A) more:** Rebecca Treiman et al., "Statistical Learning and Spelling: Older Prephonological Spellers Produce More Wordlike Spellings Than Younger Prephonological Spellers," *Child Development* 89, no. 4 (July/August 2018): e432–e438, https://doi.org/10.1111/cdev.12893https://doi.org/10.1111/cdev.12893.

159. **Letters from their own names, and letter combinations in alphabetic order, are overrepresented:** Treiman et al., "Older Prephonological Spellers," e432–440.

159. **"statistical learning":** Treiman et al., "Older Prephonological Spellers," e431–32; Rebecca Treiman, "Teaching and Learning Spelling," *Child Development Perspectives* 12, no. 4 (December 2018): 238; Rebecca Treiman, "Statistical Learning and Spelling," *Language, Speech, and Hearing Services in Schools* 49, no. 3S (August 2018): 644–648, https://doi.org /10.1044/2018_LSHSS-STLT1-17-0122.

161. **"Allowing children to engage":** Gene Ouellette and Monique Sénéchal, "Invented Spelling in Kindergarten as a Predictor of Reading and Spelling in Grade 1: A New Pathway to Literacy, or Just the Same Road, Less Known?," *Developmental Psychology* 53, no. 1 (January 2017): 85, https://doi.org/10.1037/dev0000179.

166. **a nearly universal method:** Gary Libben, Christina L. Gagné, and Wolfgang U. Dressler, "The Representation and Process of Compound Words," in *Word Knowledge and Word Usage: A Cross-Disciplinary Guide to the Mental Lexicon*, vol. 337, eds. Vito Pirrelli, Ingo Plag, and Wolfgang U. Dressler (Berlin: De Gruyter, 2020), 336–342, https://doi.org /10.1515/9783110440577.

167. **present with various spellings since Middle English:** Barry J. Blake, "Sound Symbolism in English: Weighing the Evidence," *Australian Journal of Linguistics* 37, no. 3 (2017): 290, https://doi.org/10.1080/07268602.2017.1298394.

167. **some physicians think it's time to abandon eponyms:** Alexander Woywodt and Eric Matteson, "Should Eponyms Be Abandoned? Yes," *BMJ* 335 (September 2007): 424, https://doi.org/10.1136/bmj.39308.342639.AD.

168. *portmanteaus,* **after stiff leather suitcases:** Lewis Carroll, *Alice's Adventures in Wonderland and Other Classic Works* (New York: Fall River Press, 2014), 198–199.

169. **partial lists of the knowledge and skills:** "English Language Arts Standards," Common Core States Standards Initiative, accessed January 11, 2022, http://www.corestandards.org

/ELA-Literacy; "Texas Administrative Code: Texas Essential Knowledge and Skills for English Language Arts and Reading: Elementary," Texas Education Agency, accessed January 11, 2022, https://texreg.sos.state.tx.us/public/readtac$ext.ViewTAC?tac_view =5&ti=19&pt=2&ch=110&sch=A&rl=Y; Joshi et al., "How Words Cast Their Spell"; Misty Adoniou, *Spelling It Out: How Words Work and How to Teach Them* (Cambridge, UK: Cambridge University Press, 2016), 130–131.

172. **devote considerable time:** Shalini Shankar, *Beeline: What Spelling Bees Reveal About Generation Z's New Path to Success* (New York: Hachette Book Group, 2019), chap. 5.

172. **5 years old:** Katie Kindelan, "6-Year-Old Is Youngest Competitor at the Scripps National Spelling Bee," ABC News, https://abcnews.go.com/Lifestyle/year-youngest-competitor -scripps-national-spelling-bee/story?id=47728060.

172. **hours preparing word lists and study materials:** Shankar, *Beeline*, chap. 1, 2, 5.

173. **pronouncing *righteous* as ri-tee-us:** Shankar, *Beeline*, 137–138.

173. **studied seven hours a day:** Janell Ross, "Zaila Avant-garde Knows the Troubling History behind Her Historic Spelling Bee Win," *Time*, https://time.com/6080654/zaila-avant-garde -spelling-bee-equality.

173. **"astounding progress":** Shalini Shankar, "Shankar: Zaila Avant-garde—2021 Scripps National Spelling Bee Champ—Stands Where Black Children Were Once Kept Out," *The Palm Beach Post*, July 14, 2021, https://www.palmbeachpost.com/story/opinion/columns /2021/07/14/zaila-avant-garde-2021-scripps-national-spelling-bee-champ-stands-where -black-children-were-once-kep/7944678002.

173. **spending her $10,000 prize winnings:** Ben Nuckols, "Louisiana Teen Is More Than a Spelling Bee Finalist. She's a 3x World Record Holder," NOLA.com, updated July 9, 2021, https://www.nola.com/news/article_febe1422-e02a-11eb-889f-67c4e39efe78.html.

10. EXTRA CREDIT: HOW SAVVY PARENTS KEEP LEARNING

177. **our pediatricians, relatives, and friends:** "Tuning In: Parents of Young Children Speak Up about What They Think, Know and Need," *Zero to Three*, 2016, 21, https://www .zerotothree.org/document/764.

178. **"Each one answers the question":** Kim Tingley, "How Much Alcohol Can You Drink Safely?" *New York Times*, May 16, 2019, Magazine sec., https://www.nytimes.com/2019 /05/16/magazine/how-much-alcohol-can-you-drink-safe-health.html.

179. **an average of seventeen years:** E. A. Balas and S. A. Boren, "Managing Clinical Knowledge for Health Care Improvement," *Yearbook of Medical Informatics* 09 (2000): 66, https://doi.org/10.1055/s-0038-1637943.

179. **"Practitioners want their questions answered":** Denise M. Rousseau, "A Sticky, Leveraging, and Scalable Strategy for High-Quality Connections between Organizational Practice and Science," *Academy of Management Journal* 50, no. 5 (October 2007): 1037, https://doi.org/10.5465/AMJ.2007.27155539.

179. **four studies with different methods:** Lisa S. Scott and Alexandra Monesson, "The Origin of Biases in Face Perception," *Psychological Science* 20, no. 6 (2009): 677–679, https://doi .org/10.1111%2Fj.1467-9280.2009.02348.x; Lisa S. Scott and Alexandra Monesson, "Experience-Dependent Neural Specialization During Infancy," *Neuropsychologia* 48, no. 6 (May 2010): 1858–1861, https://doi.org/10.1016/j.neuropsychologia.2010.02.008; Lisa S. Scott, "Mechanisms Underlying the Emergence of Object Representations During Infancy," *Journal of Cognitive Neuroscience* 23, no. 10 (October 2011): 2936–2943, https://doi.org/10.1162/jocn_a_00019; Charisse B. Pickron et al., "Learning to Individuate: The Specificity of Labels Differentially Impacts Infant Visual Attention," *Child Development* 89, no. 3 (May/June 2018): 700–708, https://doi.org/10.1111/cdev.13004.

180. **mini-sitcom public service announcement:** New America, "Read the Right Books at the Right Time: A Learning Sciences Exchange Fellows' Project," YouTube video, 8:37, https://www.youtube.com/watch?v=UtNANpAyQOw.

180. **picked up in media:** Lisa S. Scott, "Brain Study Suggests the Type of Book You Read to Your Baby Is Important," *Washington Post*, December 31, 2017, Health and Science sec., https://www.washingtonpost.com/national/health-science/brain-study-suggests-the-type-of -book-you-read-to-your-baby-is-important/2017/12/29/c1cec97e-ea5d-11e7-9f92 -10a2203f6c8d_story.html; Lisa Scott, "Lisa Scott: For Baby's Brain to Benefit, Read the Right Books at the Right Time," *New Zealand Herald*, December 10, 2017, https://www .nzherald.co.nz/lifestyle/lisa-scott-for-babys-brain-to-benefit-read-the-right-books-at-the -right-time/7LO2YRJJ25BB6UHMMW2MNKBBCA.

182. **an aha moment:** Lisa Oakes, "Representing Babies in Science: How We Describe Our Samples Is Important," *The International Congress of Infant Studies Baby Blog*, June 1, 2021, https://infantstudies.org/representing-babies-in-science-how-we-describe-our-samples -is-important.

183. **"it used to seem implausible":** Oakes, "Representing Babies."

183. **real differences in the environments and experiences:** Oakes, "Representing Babies."

CONCLUSION: RAISING ALL READERS

192. **Lucy Goode Brooks:** John T. Kneebone and the *Dictionary of Virginia Biography*, "Lucy Goode Brooks (1818–1900)," *Encyclopedia Virginia*, http://www.EncyclopediaVirginia.org /Brooks_Lucy_Goode_1818-1900.

Index